MW01610419

Stages of Personal Maturity

In Search of Self

John D. Reimers

Llumina Press

© 2006 John D. Reimers

All rights reserved. No part of this publication may be reproduced or transmitted in any form or by any means electronic or mechanical, including photocopy, recording, or any information storage and retrieval system, without permission in writing from both the copyright owner and the publisher.

Requests for permission to make copies of any part of this work should be mailed to Permissions Department, Llumina Press, PO Box 772246, Coral Springs, FL 33077-2246

ISBN: 1-59526-614-3   PB
        1-59526-615-1   E-book

Printed in the United States of America by Llumina Press

Library of Congress Control Number: 2006907791

Stages of
Personal Maturity

Introduction

In the beginning, the human race began a sojourn in the earth in physical form. We have been struggling with this journey ever since. It doesn't really seem to matter exactly how we became, but more important, what we are becoming. It seems that human's struggle to find themselves has certainly not been of the utmost importance, as human's have been struggling for physical survival since our beginning. Even today, human's are struggling for their existence. We seem to find little time to search for our true self. Understanding our existence is left to others. Growing through life's problems is the reality we all face each and every day. We do exist.

The idea of this book came about as a result of my own personal experiences, observations and relationships with people.

In Search of Self. It is meant to be a guide in the journey of searching for our true self. It is my hope that it becomes a treasure map, somewhat complicated, full of symbols, hard to find, one that will take a long journey for some. The treasure you can find will be the greatest available to us – the knowledge and understanding of your true nature. You can have the ability to function in the most mature way.

Maturity gives us freedom; unlocks the chains that have bound us to the earth. It opens our vision of our true self, gives us the direction and the autonomy to control the world in which we live. Maturity enables us to use our lives in service to other people. Full maturity is a journey that is becoming a true individualization of the Love that created us.

There have been so many times that I truly feel that the human race has not evolved very far. Reading of the many tragedies in our newspapers and listening to the barbaric, cruel and evil events across the world strikes a tone of despair in me. I am concerned for the future of the human race. We are all attached in some way or another. Being dependent upon each other for survival, it is paramount that we continue to search for our loving self. We must shed the chains of self-indulgence, hatred and anger – the dark side from which we have come – toward a more loving glow of warm light that shines down on us from our Creator.

The first part of this book deals with a theory that I have developed that I call *Stages of Personal Maturity*. I first became aware of the research on development of self by reading Jane Lovinger's work on ego development. It gave me a foundation in which to observe myself as well as the people I worked with in order to understand their motives and behavior. Since that time, I have developed a more comprehensive, complete concept of maturity that follows six stages. It is these stages that have been the foundation for my own understanding of myself. These stages are meant to be a guideline for one's self. It is through this roadmap that we can judge ourselves. We can see how far we have come in our own maturity. We must do this on a daily basis. It is often difficult and painful for humans to self-evaluate and to grow.

I think it is important for one to know where they are in order to move forward. When one believes that he is on the top of the hill but he has only begun his climb, he may rest there, not seeking or searching for the higher peaks that are above him.

Stages of Personal Maturity is an attempt to identify behaviors and characteristics of people who function at different levels of maturity. In exploring them, it is my hope that we will be able to identify our own behaviors. Seeing the need for growth, *Stages of Personal Maturity* will guide us towards the mature self. It will give you a loving power.

These stages were developed from my many observations as a school principal and counselor. Through evaluation of people's performance and through many conferences with students, parents and staff, a pattern of behavior was observed. I employed a single organism-reaching model, learned behavior and patterns of ten selected adults over a period of five years. Change in adults seems to be difficult and almost impossible at times. Yet, some adults' growth comes quite quickly with little direction. *Stages of Personal Maturity* is an attempt to answer questions about our behavior and the roadblocks that limit our success in our workplace, home and community.

Stages of Personal Maturity is not meant to be a concept that is used to label or judge other people, but a yardstick to measure our own behavior in relationship to our maturity. It is my hope that if we know where we are, what we want, and what direction we should be going, then we know where our journey must lead us.

This book is entitled *In Search of <u>Self,</u>* NOT *In Search of <u>Others</u>,* however, it can be helpful to understand other people in our lives so that we can help them. If we can display empathy and understanding for relationships we have, then we can find ways to help each other grow and mature. Our purpose must be how we can serve others: accept them, love them and remove the judgment that we so often place on our closest loved ones.

The chapters which follow *Stages of Personal Maturity* are ideas and techniques which I have used over the years to initiate change within myself and with the people I have worked with in the areas of counseling.

The chapter of parenting comes from my experiences as a principal working with elementary students and parents as well as from the greatest challenge – working with my own two sons. I know there are many parents out there who struggle each day with relationships with their children and mates. The chapter on parenting is an attempt to give some guidance and assistance in this sometimes-difficult process.

It is one thing to identify where we are; it is another to try to discover ways to help us grow and mature. In the transition chapter, there are many ideas and activities that can help us make transitions to higher stages of maturity. I will cover many of the ideas I have used in my own life or that have been successful when working with other people.

When we are young, we are most interested in our relationships. It is a time for discovery and for involvement, which is extremely important to our own development. The chapter on young love is intended to help the young person with his/her own maturity in relationship to the struggles, joys and pitfalls of an intimate relationship. Relationships are extremely important in our life. It is important that we are able to judge those relationships and ourselves as we enter into those that can affect us over our entire life.

Chapter 4 is devoted to marriage and divorce. It seems that almost everyone at one time or other becomes in a relationship that, at some point, ends. Through those relationships comes our opportunity to grow, to become close to people and to be able to analyze ourselves in relationship to the person with whom we have joined ourselves.

Chapter 5 deals with employment. Many people are successful in the workplace because of their ability to be patient and responsible. Yet there are others who continue to fail time after time. This again has a very close relationship to the individual's level of maturity. This chapter is my attempt to assist people to be successful in their jobs. Employers need to be able to search for the best employees, especially in the field of education. It is my desire and strong belief to have the best people possible working with children in the area of education. *Stages of Personal Maturity* can help.

If we are to grow as a society, we need the best role models to educate our children. We need the nurturing, mature person in those classrooms. I have been very successful using the maturity stages while hiring, evaluating and developing my own staff over the past 20 years. I share my experiences and ideas with those of you who want to improve your organization.

Chapter 6 – Death and Dying – is a natural sequence of life and yet, too often, people do not think about this aspect until they are faced with it. They tend to bury the loss in their subconscious and do not deal with it directly. This is a chapter in which the loss of a loved one, and some ideas about the death experience, are discussed.

Chapter 7 is probably the most important chapter of all, as it deals with the power of the universe that has created all of us. We call it by many names, Light of love, the Creator, God the Father. God is the unconditional Love that created us, sustains, us, and that we are truly searching for by returning to that love by becoming mature.

In the conclusion, I will try to make sense out of the entire book and hopefully, give direction to those who have taken the time to read it. I have included exercise techniques that can be used in meditation and prayer. This practice can help us move through our own stages of maturity toward the end of our quest, which is an understanding and knowledge of "self" and our relationship to our Creator.

In writing this book, I have tried not to over-intellectualize the concepts. Instead, I have tried to make them clear and straightforward in a common language so that all people seeking will understand them. I have tried not to create a lot of new jargon that may be difficult for people to understand. I do not want readers to have to learn a whole new language in order to understand the concepts presented.

I believe the concepts are not unique to me, but are universal in nature. Many people who are seeking have come up with the same thoughts. I have organized the thoughts in this manner, enabling people to find an interpretation that may fit with their own individual lives. Perhaps this may guide them toward a richer understanding of the world they live in and of themselves.

This book is an adventure. It will be challenging. May you have the patience to endure the intellectual thought that it will take to read it. May your heart feel the love from which it is written. I hope it will guide you and help you find a richer and fuller life. So many books are purchased, a few chapters read, and then laid aside. You and the entire human race will grow and mature though higher levels of awareness if we have the courage to search for ourselves. Through a newfound maturity, the world will be stronger. This new maturity will enable us to solve the problems of the world. People will seek to serve each other. The whole human race will continue to grow. Many of the problems of famine, hunger, starvation and homelessness will be solved when people seek to serve each other. We have been given an unlimited resource to use: an energy that is beyond belief, yet, we have not fully tapped into the energy that could create a world of joy and love. You can find and use this power.

For each positive or negative action we take, there is a profound ripple effect on the lives of many people. On September 11, 2001, a very small number of people profoundly affected the lives of over 2000 individuals and their families and friends, as well as citizens of almost every nation in the world when the planes were hijacked and flown into the World Trade Center, the Pentagon and the field in Pennsylvania. May our actions have a positive ripple effect on those around us and the entire world.

Table of Contents

PART I

Stages of Personal Maturity

Chapter 1

The Egotist Stage

The first stage of personal maturity is probably the most difficult for me to discuss or examine. It is the darkest hurting side which is evil incarnate in our world. Yet is it so important that we not ignore the egotists of our world, for they are the ones who truly do us harm and keep our whole race from growing. The egotists are the collective commissioners of evil.

The stages of development are natural in young children. For some reason, the egotist as an adult has remained at that early stage of self-confinement, of only seeing himself, and the world only relates to him. He does not fit into the broader sense of the world but in his own world. It is a lonely, self-indulging world. The models we have for egotists are found in our newspapers and news reports everyday. Our history is full of egotists who brought great harm to mankind.

I will discuss several aspects of each stage beginning with the function of character. The emotional stance that an egotist takes is one of being very impulsive. He never thinks, but only reacts to his needs. There is extreme fear that comes over him directing him in his actions. His orientation is toward self-interest. He is very judgmental against the world if it does not fit his own personal needs. This self-interest is in all aspects – from what he eats, to whom he relates, to what type of job he may try to hold.

This person shows a great deal of irresponsibility and usually cannot hold a job. We find this character in our prisons and in our mental institutions. Society tries to deal with the egotist's extreme negative behavior by confining them and taking them out of the mainstream of life. Their relational style is one of systematically being selfish. Any event in life has to serve the self. There is much hatred. Any emotional trauma can trigger hate which spills out at the world and people around them. They tend to be very aggressive and easily angered. It comes from a repressed anger like a soda bottle being shaken. Anyone who comes along and slips the top off gets the full force of the shaken soda bottle. They are very hostile because they cannot feel any empathy. They can become violent at any moment.

At the elementary level we find that the egotist is a child who usually becomes the school-yard bully. He can only blame the other child for his actions and only wants to hurt other children. Afterward he feels no remorse for his actions and will not take responsibility. He cannot see how another person could feel hurt and pain. The egocentric way is very natural in a two year-old, but is very dangerous in a third grader or an adult.

An egotist may be highly intelligent, yet there is great interference with the use of the intellect, for actions are driven by impulses rather than by thoughtfulness. The egotist is controlled by feelings and desires that are triggered by emotions laden by memories. Throughout this book we will discuss how an egotist became an egotist and remained so. It is important in parenting and in nurturing that we understand how we can move from this stage.

The cognitive style of an egotist displays extreme conceptual confusion. If you ever talk with an egotist, you cannot understand their thinking – it is not rational but confused and the concepts are turned around in order so that the person can manipulate situation in order to feel safe and comfortable. It is very difficult to have a rational discussion with a person at this level. The person uses stereotypes, clichés, and generalizations that will not speak to specific ideas or enable you to make sense form them. The person is very subjective, only viewing the world from his viewpoint. He will not be able to see your side of a conflict or discussion. This brings a person to become very illogical. This does not fall into sequence unless they serve the self. This person will not show common sense because they cannot think in a logical way.

The intuition that many of us use is blocked at this egotistical stage. The feelings and desires block the intuition from coming forth to guide the person in their life. The person's life focus is physical. He is concerned only about his physical welfare and the needs that he has. He seeks pleasures only for himself. He will avoid pain at any cost to the self, yet may inflict it on others randomly and eagerly. He is obsessed with his sexuality. He believes he is the supreme authority in his world and anyone who doesn't conform to his world is expendable. For him, those immediate needs must be met at all times and all other people or situations must give way to his desires. He truly sees only himself.

In the chapters on parenting, we will discuss how a child who should go through this stage has stayed at a very self-centered egotistical level of maturity.

True historical supreme egotists who have affected many people are Adolph Hitler, Ted Bundy and Charles Manson. We can read about many others each day. I take this time to discuss two of them briefly only to give a model of what an egotist looks like in our own time.

If you examine Adolph Hitler, you see a person who is so self-confined and so caught up in his own grandeur that he became very controlling and used his intellect to manipulate a world. He destroyed millions of lives based on a lack of empathy or concern for another person. If he could dehumanize the Jew down to a common housefly that could be swatted away and destroyed, his self-confined egotistical self would allow him to manipulate people and commit the world's atrocities that took place during World War II. The control and the effect that he had over the world should never be forgotten. I am thankful for the many books, movies and ideas that keep the knowledge of such a person alive for there are many egotists out there who could become as controlling and as devastating as Adolph Hitler.

Adolph Hitler was at the right time and at the right place. He did not have enough mature people around him to stop him. An egotist is very controlling and can destroy a great deal before he is stopped.

Charles Manson, on the other hand, probably had moved into the transitional stage between the egotist and the self-confined stage, which is the next stage that I will discuss. He was able to manipulate other people to do his bidding by controlling them, being deceitful and by being dishonest. He is truly evil of incarnate because of his ability to blame other races, wanting to start a civil war within our country, and thinking so very illogically that he played his thoughts out.

It is fortunate that in America an egotist was stopped short. In some underdeveloped countries we still have egotists running rampant over their country creating death squads and human rights are at very low ebb.

Chapter 2

The Self-Confined Stage

It is not my intent to dwell long on some of the models I present as the important is not to judge others but to look at behaviors within ourselves. As the
egotist moves into transition, he remains self-confined. He still has many negative behaviors, yet is more capable of living in society. At times he conforms to
the rules and regulations but only as they suit the self.

The function of character of a self-confined person would be opportunistic –
always taking the opportunity to fulfill the self's needs. Also very fearful, he
lacks a sense of purpose or meaning in his life. He aimlessly wanders only trying to fulfill the immediate needs. He is very self-protective. If one confronts
him, he will draw back and lash out in a self-protective manner.

Any actions that a self-confined person takes and is caught doing would
cause him immediately to blame it on another person or situation. We find this
often in young children, yet they usually learn to take responsibility and grow
out of this. The adult who remains self-confined will continue to blame the government, the rules, the regulations, other people, the situation – anything but
take responsibility for his own actions. We see these people in our work places.
In some instances they may live next door. You probably never speak to this
person as they are easily angered, irresponsible, and hard to get along with.

The character of a self-confined person is very sneaky and deceptive. He may
come across as very friendly and helpful in the beginning, but only acts that way
to set up an opportunity to gain from you. He uses other people for his gain.

These people are usually found out after several encounters. Their relational style is one of manipulation. They will manipulate the world to get their way. The manipulations are in order to continue their own self-indulgence. They are able to distort their world and do not have a clear accurate picture of the world in which they live. They are moved by a great deal of mistrust. This person, for instance, would not want to be evaluated in a situation at work. They could possibly become angry and blame others if you ask them to improve. They may quit or become rebellious and undermine your authority. They are easily provoked and become incensed at any activity with does not go their way. They can be very abusive and neglectful. We see this abusive person on the news reports every night concerning child abuse and domestic violence. Domestic violence and child abuse are national problems that we read about daily.

The self-confined person is able to inflict abuse and neglect on the people around him. He may be in a relationship through manipulations – using sneaky and deceptive ways to lure the person in. They he may turn on the person, showing no empathy and becoming very abusive. This person lacks structure in his life. He does not have boundaries. He does not have guidelines in which to conform. Anything and everything is okay as long as he initiates it, however not if it is initiated by someone else.

The self-confined person is very exploitive. He will exploit the situation to his own good at all costs. He seeks to be served by others. As long as his needs are served, he will respond in kind. His intellect is interfered with by his stage of maturity. They are seen as the doer. They will do what they are told only to survive. They do not think about or understand their motives. They are impulsive in order to take care of the basic needs that they have. Again, their intellect is controlled by feelings and desires deep inside their subconscious.

The self-confined person's cognitive style is still of conceptual confusion. They continue to use stereotypes and clichés, never hitting on specific information. They are persistently subjective and very defensive. This stage is noted by a continual lack of common sense. Their emotions and intuitions are blocked by feelings and desires that they do not understand and cannot control. Their life focus is undisciplined and inconsistent. They are concerned with material possessions and have wishful fantasies. There is no clear reality, there are not goals and they aimlessly wander – relating only to things that can give them immediate gratification.

Many self-confined people are drawn toward alcohol and drug abuse. This continues to meet their immediate needs but traps them in their own confined world. This person continues to control his own little world and sees himself first. He sometimes can see other people in his life but usually only in relationship to how and what they can do for him.

Chapter 3

The Conventional Stage

The next stage of maturity is the conventional stage. This is the stage where we find most adults. These adults reach this stage in their late teens and never grow beyond it.

The conventional maturity level is characterized by the ability to conform to standards and laws that society has placed on us. People at this level are able to fit within the structure of society and are very successful. They are still very close to the self-confined stage in their behaviors and, at times, can revert to those lower self-serving stages.

The conventional person is characterized by reluctance. They are very unsure of themselves. They remain within their conventional society yet are reluctant to go beyond; to push themselves; to have a vision of what could be. They do not yet set goals that are attainable beyond their daily needs. They still display some fear and are fretful. They conform to society's established practices and want very much to be accepted by others. They can be very testy because they are unsure of themselves, but they are responsible, for the most part. They can hold down jobs, and are seen as the major work force in our country. They can be controlled by other people; either the lower, self-confined person who is very manipulative and opportunistic, or a "conscious" person who has vision and can direct them. They are not seen as leaders. They are followers.

The conventional person tends to find the easy way out and be expedient in meeting his own needs first. Sometimes they will display a superficial niceness in order to have their needs met. They continue to be self-indulgent and would distort information and ideas in order to protect themselves. There is still much mistrust at this level for the motives of other people, yet they are manipulated. They too, can be abusive and neglectful but are usually not as harsh or an angry as the self-confined person. They have grown out of the total self-confined stage and are now aware of a bigger world and their part in it. They will continue to conform to group norms and have a very strong desire to belong – however, only because they believe it is expected, not because they understand the whole picture.

The conventional person will seek out organizations to belong to in order to feel a part of something for there is a strong need to be a part of a group and be accepted. They are still the 'doers'. They do what is expected of them without thinking and without questioning. They would still seek to be served by others rather than growing and able to give to others. They do not have the energy for anyone else unless it fits in the conformity of what is expected of them. They too can be controlled by their own feelings and desires that are triggered by the emotions from the memories of their own childhood.

The conventional person's cognitive style is conceptual simplicity. They can see things simplistically but not in depth. There is a subjective/objective tug of war in their lives. Seeing the other person's side is possible, but they continue to move back to the safe more self-confined stage of looking at it from their own point of view first because it is less risky. They are sometimes illogical, but usually they can use common sense and function in the world and get along. There is no use of their intuition. They are not aware of that, as they are not thinking for themselves other than to maintain their conformity to the established group rules. Their appearance is of main concern, as they want to be accepted. Social acceptability is a prime life focus: they want to fit in. They are consumers of goods for this reason. It is possible for them to see other people in certain conditions, yet they will still see themselves first.

If you see yourself as a conventional person as you are reading, then you are probably the person who can be most helped by this book for it is the person who has reached the conventional stage that, with help and understanding, can use this as a roadmap and can make that transition to the consciousness level. Because the majority of people have reached this conventional stage, it is my hope and intent that through a better understanding and a healing of some of those memories a person will grow. In the later transitional chapters of this book, the conventional person will be the one who can most benefit from the exercises and from the willingness to want to mature. Most adults have reached the conventional stage but remain there throughout their entire life and never grow beyond.

Chapter 4

The Conscious Stage

The conscious stage is an exciting and wonderful level. A few adults reach this in their 20's. The experiences that have taken place in their lives have helped them mature. They have been nurtured and loved throughout their life. They have grown through an awareness of not only themselves but a bigger world – one that is more complex and interesting. Tapping the resources of energy they can use it no only for taking care of their own needs, for that almost becomes automatic, but they have the energy to serve others and make a difference in our world. They are the role models that we look up to. They are the people who are leaders in a positive way. Making our world a better place in which to live is their focus.

This is a most exciting stage because it displays much joy and energy. The function of this person's character is very conscientious. He is concerned about himself and his fellow man. He selects ideals, has goals and is very calm. The long-term goals are set and he strives toward them. He has a vision of what can take place and sets about working towards the completion of the vision. This person is successful because he is able to evaluate his own actions. He sees and understands the people around him. In this self-evaluation he can self-correct and make changes that are necessary for him to be successful.

He is very forgiving of himself and others, for when he does make a mistake, he understands that he must forgive and forget and move forward. He also forgives the people around him and is not laden with any heavy memories of hurt or anger, yet is joyful in his responses to people in his life. He is a very responsible person who is concerned about his behavior and his actions and will take responsibility for them.

In his relational style he is conscientious, empathetic, and concerned about others. His empathy is displayed in his family life and his work place. He is concerned about others. He can put himself in the other person's shoes and is able to understand his needs as well as his own. He provides positive structure and moral values in his life and has set boundaries. He would not stray to take drugs or use alcohol, for he feels no need. He builds rapport with people intentionally because he enjoys them and wants to help them.

A major step in the transition from the conventional stage to the conscious stage is seeking to serve others. Now he has the energy to help other people and seeks to serve them. His intellect is no longer interfered with by emotions and feelings. The intellectual potential is starting to be revealed. This person is a thinker who will think about himself, the world that he lives in, and his abilities. He will apply his abilities to his situation. He is governed by reason and rightness. He understands what is right for him in relationship to a broader world. His conceptual ideas are complex. He can think of many things and he can see many relationships. He cannot only just see his own world but see himself in a broader complex world. He has much tolerance for ambiguity, as everything is not black or white. He can see the uniqueness of people and the different needs of people. He is not prejudiced.

The conscious person is very objective. He can remove himself from situations and decisions and can see it from viewpoints other than his own. He is logical. The order and the nature of the world have been revealed to him. He sees that there is harmony and that there are natural laws. Displaying a great deal of common sense, he can make decisions quickly, and can react in positive ways. Using his own intuition, he listens to it, and lets it guide him in his life.

This person attains a great deal of mutual achievements, enjoys being part of a team, enjoys accomplishing goals set and has a great deal of self-respect and respect for other people. The faith that he has toward himself and his fellow man guides him. Faith is his life's focus. He is aware of his needs and the needs of others, and he can take care of himself and help others. He reaps energy by serving others that he uses to contribute to the world.

The conscious person is at a friendly, helpful, exciting level of maturity, one that is fulfilled in many ways. We have all known people at this level. They are the people that we look up to and respect. They are also the people we say have control of their life and are very successful.

Chapter 5

The Autonomous Stage

As a person moves to an autonomous state, they become more authentic, more true to their nature. They are loving, able to manage conflict very easily and have much patience. Although this person is rare, I believe I have known several in my life and continue to seek to understand the autonomous person. Throughout history we have many examples of those who were autonomous.

The autonomous person displays a great deal of strength and courage. They are self-confirmed – no long self-confined. They understand and love themselves and others. They never judge other people or situations until they have all the information but suspend judgment until all the information is in. They are very responsible to themselves and to the people that they work for.

This person can always be trusted because they are straightforward and honest. The autonomous person's relational style is very creative. The natural authentic energy flowing through him manifests itself in many creative loving ways. Grace and beauty radiates from the autonomous person. You can trust and respect this person. Unconditional love is in every aspect of their lives. They can establish automatic rapport.

Have you ever met a person who immediately establishes rapport with you, and you feel love coming from them? This has happened to me several times in my life. It is wonderful that they can establish a loving relationship immediately. Their needs are met. They are conscious of the world. Autonomy comes by using our own energy. A positive relationship will be established with you immediately and automatically. They are nurturing and loving people. They have the ability to cope in their live and solve problems almost effortlessly. They have complete empathy for the human race. Their ability to care is displayed by seeking to serve others. They are intellectually complete and their potentials are being reached. They no longer are just thinkers, but 'knowers'. They know something through their own experiences and through their own thinking process. They use their intellect to tackle the problems of our world and solve them. Their knowledge comes through their own intellect and their own experiences. Governed by truth and wisdom, they are like a light in the darkness. They have increased conceptual complexity. Having the ability to think with complexity allows them to understand the world in which they live and make sense of it. They have a very healthy objectivity. They know when they are subjective.

This autonomous maturity level gives them insight into their own world. They can understand their own subjectivity. They become skilled in logic, for the world is a logical order and they are able to see it, use it and understand it. They apply common sense throughout all their actions and ideas. They trust their own intuition and use it to guide them in their lives. Their life focus is one of discipline and consistency. They are self-fulfilled through the realization of their goals and they have integrated their service to others. Their whole life is way beyond the personal needs but has become one of serving others in many ways. This energy seems to build in them, and they are able to give it to other people through service. They see others first. As their own needs are taken care of, they will respond to the needs of others first.

If you meet or know an autonomous person, you can learn a great deal from him. He will probably be the best friend you have ever had and a relationship will probably develop that should be nurtured and developed.

Chapter 6

The Mature Stage

The last level of maturity is what I have labeled mature. Although I personally have never met a mature person, I think there are historical models to which we can look. Having been raised in a Christian family, my role model while grown up was Jesus. For other religions, it could be their prophet.

The mature are the collective consciousness of love. The mature person is one who has reached maturity in a free and full manner. He is very peaceful in his existence and continues to display a great deal of strength and courage in his convictions. His character is one of complete maturation of self. His life is a constant application of truth and natural responsibility. He takes it unconditionally and is continually giving to other people. His honesty, love and joy in his work are given at a natural level.

The person that I studied and believe fits this character was Mother Theresa of Calcutta. She truly exemplified a mature person. She was loving and caring.

The mature relational style is a natural expression of love. There is much grace and beauty about a mature person. They are affirming and joyful. They display an individualization of love for themselves and their fellow man. They are consistent in their serving, independent and cooperative and are always seeking to serve others. Their intellectual potential is reached. They are 'knowers'. They have a great deal of understanding of the truth and wisdom that is a universal knowledge. Only the most mature person can filter through this universal knowledge and use it to live a life of service.

The mature person's cognitive style is holistically complex. They see the whole very complexly yet, at times, very simply, as it is a natural for them. They have a vision of harmony and unity for all mankind. They feel a part of the whole human race simultaneously as they display empathy for others. They have a balance of subjectivity/objectivity. They see themselves in relationship to others in a natural balance. They have a great deal of depth to their thinking and are appropriately logical. They have pure and normal thought coming from their ability to balance their lives with joy and love. They have an appropriate use of their intuition. They let their intuition guide them because they are in touch with the creative source – God!

Their self-identify is very well developed. They are disciplined and consistent and at times enlightened. The truths that are spoken from a mature person truly are universal ideas and thoughts that should touch the hearts of us all. The mature person sees all simultaneously. They are no longer concerned with just themselves, but see the whole world and themselves in it all at the same time.

The mature person is admired. Most of us cannot understand how they are able to be so serving and sacrifice so much. Yet to them, it is a natural way. Their needs are met and they are peaceful. The energy that flows through them gives them strength and health. They live very joyful lives. As we struggle at the lowers levels each day, they have attained a level of maturity that all religions and philosophy seek to understand.

As I have gone through the six stages of maturity, I have listed them as behaviors and ideas, again to be a map for us to follow, a rule by which to measure ourselves – behaviors which we can identify in our own lives and other behaviors which we can replace with the negative lowers ones. At the end of this section there is a charge with the six stages and transitional stages listed on them. I have put them in the chart so that it can be used daily. I want you, the reader, to be able to reflect on the levels and use them as you continue to grow.

The chapters to come will continually relate back to the stages of maturity, so it is my hope that the chart provided will be used and understood as you read the following chapters and relate back to the stages of maturity.

STAGES OF MATURITY (left side of chart)

Transition	EGOTIST	ES	SELF-CONFINED	SV	CONVENTIONAL	VC

Function of Character:

Emotional:
- Impulsive / Extreme fear
- Opportunistic / Fearful
- Reluctant / Fretful

Orientation:
{ Lacks sense of purpose or meaning }

Self-interest	Self-protective	Self conforms to
Judgmental	Blaming	established practice
Anti-Social	Threatening	testy
Very irresponsible	Irresponsible	Usually responsible
{ Sneaky and deceptive }

Relational Style:

Purpose:
- Systematic Selfishness / Manipulative / Expedient
{ Indulgence and distortion }
Emotional Aspect: hate / Mistrust
- Aggressive — Violent — Easily provoked / Superficial
- Easily enraged / Incensed / Niceness
- Repressed anger
{ Abusive and neglectful }
- Hostility / Lacks structure / Conform to group norms
Relationship: Dependent / Exploitive / Belonging
{ Seeks to be served by others }

Intellect:
{ Intellectual Interference }
{ Doer }
{ Controlled by felings and desires triggered by emotion laden memories }

Cognitive Style:
- Extreme conceptual confusion / Conceptual confusion / Conceptual simplicity
{ se of stereotypes, cliches and generalizations }

- Extreme Subjectivity / Persistent Subjectivity Defensive / Subjective - Objective tug of war

- Extremely illogical / Illogical / Sometimes illogical
- No common sense / Lacks common sense / Usually uses common sense
{ Intuition blocked by feelings and desires } / { No use or awareness of intuition }

Life Focus:
{ Inconsistent - Undisciplined }
- Physical feelings and desires / Things, material possessions / Appearance
- Seeks pleasure / Wishful - fantasy / Social acceptability
- Avoids pain / Controls ones own little world / Uncertain
- Sexual obsessions

SEES ONLY SELF / SEES SELF 1st / SEES SELF THEN OTHERS UNDER CERTAIN CONDITIONS

STAGES OF MATURITY right side of chart

CONSCIOUS ———————— AUTONOMOUS ———————— MATURE

CA   AM

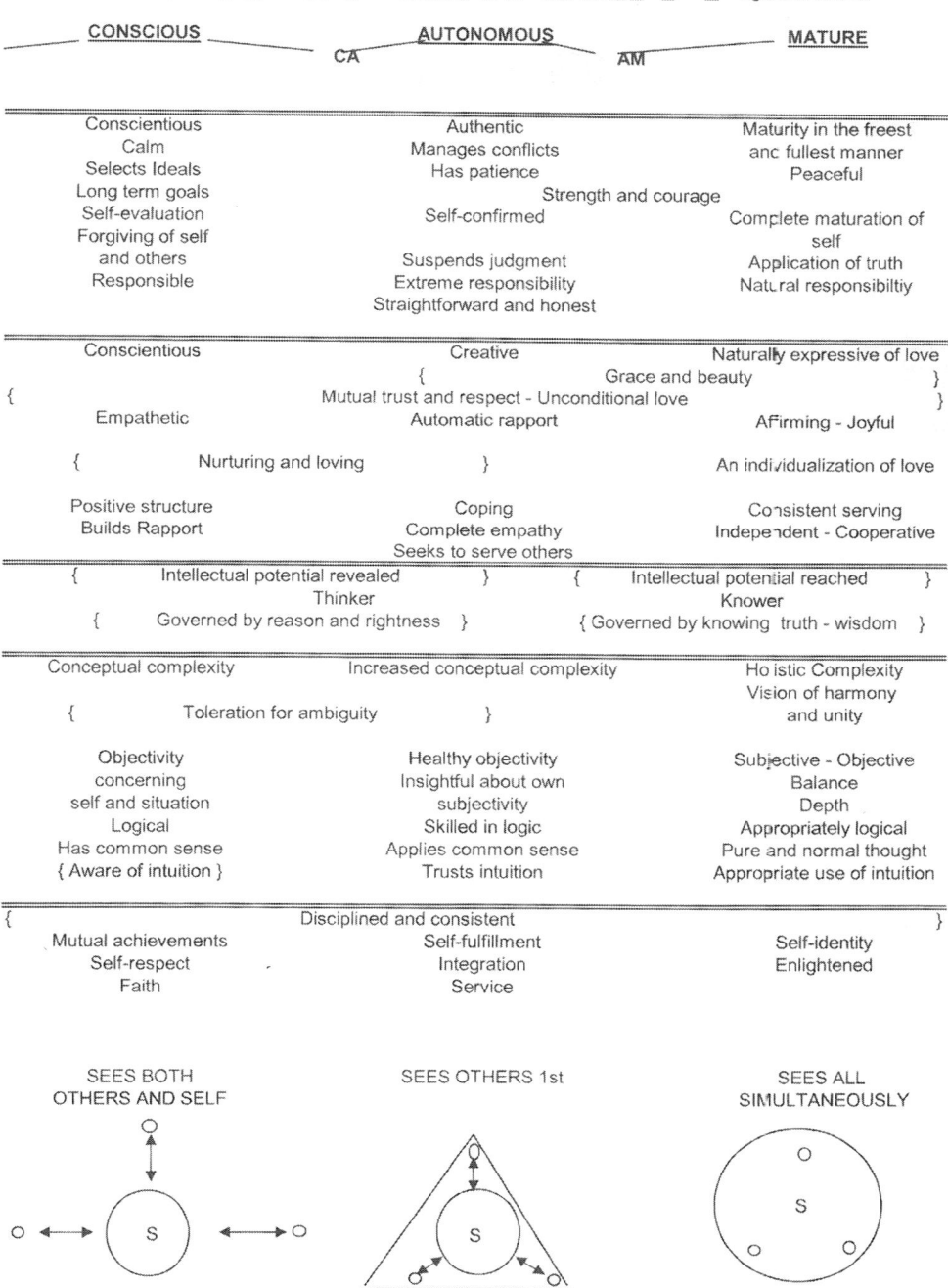

Conscientious	Authentic	Maturity in the freest
Calm	Manages conflicts	anc fullest manner
Selects Ideals	Has patience	Peaceful
Long term goals	Strength and courage	
Self-evaluation	Self-confirmed	Complete maturation of
Forgiving of self		self
and others	Suspends judgment	Application of truth
Responsible	Extreme responsibility	Natural responsibiltiy
	Straightforward and honest	

Conscientious — Creative — Naturally expressive of love

{ Grace and beauty }

{ Mutual trust and respect - Unconditional love }

Empathetic — Automatic rapport — Afirming - Joyful

{ Nurturing and loving } — An individualization of love

Positive structure — Coping — Consistent serving
Builds Rapport — Complete empathy — Independent - Cooperative
— Seeks to serve others —

{ Intellectual potential revealed } { Intellectual potential reached }
Thinker — Knower
{ Governed by reason and rightness } { Governed by knowing truth - wisdom }

Conceptual complexity — Increased conceptual complexity — Holistic Complexity
— — Vision of harmony
{ Toleration for ambiguity } — and unity

Objectivity	Healthy objectivity	Subjective - Objective
concerning	Insightful about own	Balance
self and situation	subjectivity	Depth
Logical	Skilled in logic	Appropriately logical
Has common sense	Applies common sense	Pure and normal thought
{ Aware of intuition }	Trusts intuition	Appropriate use of intuition

{ Disciplined and consistent }

Mutual achievements	Self-fulfillment	Self-identity
Self-respect	Integration	Enlightened
Faith	Service	

SEES BOTH   SEES OTHERS 1st   SEES ALL
OTHERS AND SELF   SIMULTANEOUSLY

23

PART II

In Search of Self

Chapter 1

Parenting

It is my firm belief that maturity in each of us comes about through the nurturing we received from our parents. Parenting is probably the most important aspect that can bring together all the resources needed to mature a child through the many stages in growth experiences that one encounters in their life. The task of parenting is at times difficult, stressful and almost seems impossible. It is beyond me how so many single parents survive the task.

The natural order that says that a male and female come together and produce a child would also say that it takes the two of them in harmony to mature this child. Yet each year in our society the two-parent family is becoming the minority.

As we discuss the role of parenting, we will look into the many important aspects of this unique relationship that we call 'family'. Let's begin with the birth process.

When a child is born he is brought into the world with a unique and distinct personality of his own – ready to grow and mature in an environment in which he has seemed to be drawn to. If the child is born into a loving, nurturing family, chances are that the child will grow strong in his self-concept and in his maturity.

All babies seem to be welcomed into this world with love and joy. Depending on the maturity level of the parents the child may be greeted by a parent who has either matured to the level of responsibility to take on the great task or nurturing, or not. A mature person will teach and love the child. The child may be greeted by a parent who is in a self-confined stage of maturity and is angry. This parent perhaps lacks structure, purpose and meaning – which are so necessary in parenting. Both children born into each of these families will take on may of the aspects of their parents. Each child will grow towards the potential of the role model they seek to emulate.

Let us first examine the needs of the child as he goes through those early years - comparing them to the two sets of parents described above: one set that has not matured beyond the self-confined stage and another set that has emerged into a conscious level.

Both parents instinctively want to love and care for their child, yet though their own maturity level they may or may not be able to provide the things that a child needs. The self-confined parent that is still fearful and lacks the sense of purpose and meaning may find it difficult to conform to the rigorous tasks of caring for a child 24 hours a day, seven days a week, through ear infections, colds, teething, potty training and all the other early childhood milestones. However, the conscious parents who are calm have ideals, are conscientious, see the child first. They are forgiving, responsible and will work through the rigors of child rearing.

The self-confined parent will be angered easily and at times project his hatred and anger onto the child. The self-confined parent is characterized as indulgent. This parent does not see the world in its true form because of the small world that he or she exists in. This parent will provide a world of inconsistency for the child, be unsure of himself and at the critical times in his life will pull further into his own little world. It will be difficult for the child to mature through the many stages of maturity.

I have worked with many elementary-aged students. I have observed two parenting styles that significantly hinder a child's ability to move through the levels of personal maturity. The first is neglect or abuse.

The self-confined parents, who are so caught up in their own world, will often build to the point that one or the other parent may have already left the family. Because of their impulsiveness, they may seek other opportunities. This parent does not have the patience to remain behind to take full responsibility for their parenting. This person will search aimlessly through the world, and may not even take part in the family. Left alone is a single parent who tries to make sense out of a world of loneliness and despair. When the other parent comes back into the picture, there is a possibility of neglect and abuse.

This is an all-too-frequent scene in our society today. This neglect and abuse causes the young child to remain self-confined. The child will not be able to move any farther. The reason for remaining at a self-confined stage is due to the fact that the world is viewed as harsh. Experiences that are inconsistent confuse the child. Whenever the child makes a move, there may be a lashing out, a punishment for behavior, uncertainty and a lack of love. This causes the child to be mistrusting, and manipulative – attempting to avoid the punishment by deceit, lying or blaming, and other ways to get away from the blaming parent.

The aspect of neglect leaves emptiness in the child for the child needs the unconditional love of both parents, male and female, which helps that child to grow totally in his/her relationship. As each of us has to relate to males and females in our lives, we pattern those future relationships after our first relationships with our parents. If we had a loving, accepting father, it is easy for us to accept and get along with other males. If we are female, it is easy for us to get along with females if our mothers were nurturing and caring. But if we had a father who neglected us or who was not at home then we are uncertain about males. It is often the hurt within us during our early years that cause us pain as an adult. We may have never had the experience of unconditional love.

The self-confined maturity level also has an attribute of lacking structure. Children need structure and organization in their life during the early years to know the boundaries – to know how far they can go. Having had boundaries and structure helps move us toward the conventional stage.

If there are no laws or structure within the family, then the child's boundaries are wide open. The child must aimlessly wander trying to find them. He may become very exploitive of others. Desperately, he seems to find the structure that will lead him toward meaning and purpose in his life. It is very difficult to bring a child out of the self-confined stage when there has been much abuse and neglect during those early years. Since the adult has feelings and desires which are triggered by emotion-laden memories, he lays those same emotions and memories onto his children and it becomes a vicious cycle. Statistically we know that children are abused by parents who themselves have been abused, and the vicious cycle goes on and on.

There is help for the adult who wants to move out of the self-confined stage. Techniques are discussed in the chapter on Transition.

The second cause for children to remain at the lower levels of maturity is indulgence. Many parents equate love with material gifts. The parents also allow the child to do what he wants. They are not at a level where they can provide the structure necessary for the child, so they indulge the child out of what they think is love. Yet indulgence is not love. Indulgence comes from insecurity within the person to provide the proper structure for the child to grow.

We have all seen the indulged child – the spoiled brat, the child who gets everything he wants when he wants it. That child has learned that his world can be controlled. He controls his mother and father by temper tantrums or fits or anything to get his way. What he truly wants is structure and guidance and not indulgence. Indulgence is the key to children who become manipulative, sneaky and deceptive in any way they can in order to get the things they want. It is a power struggle between them and their parents, and the continuation of indulgence only causes the child to remain in his own small world, not able to see others unless it serves him.

Having worked with many indulged children at school, it is very difficult for authority to give guidance to the child who has become so strong in his own systematic ways of seeking to fulfill his own selfish needs. A child will remain opportunistic, fearful and will lack a sense purpose or meaning, as he is only to serve himself. He will be very blaming – not taking responsibility for his actions – as that would not meet his needs.

Often in dysfunctional families, we find both indulgence and abuse. These extremes are very detrimental to the growth of the child.

If the child has been provided structure and boundaries, the child will move forward as we see in the characteristics in the conscious level of maturity. The conscious parent provides consistency, structure, purpose and meaning. The conscious person separates the child from the behavior, continues to love the child unconditionally, has a great amount of empathy and concern for his needs, but does not indulge the child's behavior. The conscious parent will have strong rapport with his children and will care about them a great deal. This parent will provide the structure necessary for growth. The conscious person will tolerate the child's temper tantrums and know that they will pass, but will not give in to the many demands of the young child. He will provide all the necessary needs that the child has. This positive structure provides boundaries for the child to test. He will find that there is an end and that the child will then conform to the necessary values of the parent.

The conscious parent is a thinker. He will think of ways of resolving the child's problem, yet will keep the child feeling safe and secure – controlling the child's behavior – therefore allowing the child to mature in a natural way. He will not abuse the child in any way, for he has patience, is calm, does not react to the behavior of the learning child, but responds to the needs of the child. Being a very conscientious person, he will look out for the needs of the child in a way that is productive and healthful.

The conscious person also anticipates the needs of the growing child, responds to them, and is prepared for them as they move through the many stages that a child goes through. To give you an example of how the two levels of maturity may solve a problem, I will tell you about a situation that comes up early in childhood, about the age of 2, when the child is ready to control his world.

The child has chosen oatmeal for breakfast. Oatmeal is fixed and set before the child. The child then sees older brother who has just come down and chosen Cheerios. The younger child wants Cheerios now rather than Oatmeal and begins to cry. After about 5 minutes, the self-confined parent gets angry, storms about, and grabs the oatmeal away. He throws some Cheerios in a bow and gives to the child. The child has learned that through a temper tantrum he gets his way. The angry parent, although angry, will still provide the needs that the child wanted immediately.

The conscious parent, however, will know that it is important for the child to live with the consequences of choice so the child can take responsibility. Even though the child may continue to scream, a conscious parent would not indulge the behavior but calmly and quietly say, "Not to worry, you can choose Cheerios tomorrow," and leave the oatmeal in front of the child. The child may scream for a long time, yet at some point, the screaming and yelling will stop, and the child will conform and begin to eat.

I used this example because my youngest son did this when he was about two years old and it actually took 45 minutes of screaming before he stopped and began to eat his oatmeal. Through the whole time I remained empathetic and caring for the person, yet did not indulge his behavior. The conventional stage of maturity would be marked by a 'vacillation between the two parenting styles."

If you analyze carefully the stages of maturity, you will find things within yourself that ring true to your own upbringing. Look closely at your own parenting skills. If you are not yet a parent, will you be ready when the time comes? It is very important for a young couple who desire to have children to analyze their own maturity, their own skills and abilities to cope with this great change that comes about by bringing a child into the world. It is a learning experience for a family and is an important one, for it is the child who can bring growth within us. It is that child who helps us dig down in our own self-evaluations. We need to take a hard and close look at our own parenting skills – look at how our parents raised us – and change what might not have worked. If you are thinking of becoming a parent, be ready for the challenge of your life.

Parents is an exciting, wonderful time, and as the years go by, the hard work, love and the care you have given to this maturing child will bring forth many wonderful returns. It is my hope that as parents read this chapter they can identify within themselves their own reactions and behaviors to situations. If your own behavior is at the lower end of the maturity scales, you can replace them with the higher level reactions and become aware of the necessity and importance of responding at a more mature stage.

It is important to note that all of us are capable, for moments of time, to revert to our lower selves. We can act irresponsibly and become angry for a moment. The important thing is that we can evaluate that anger and move away from it. We must be forgiving of ourselves and others. Taking responsibility for our own behavior and our own parenting skills is necessary. We must daily analyze where that anger and hurt comes from, always giving forgiveness so that we can move through the anger to make sure it doesn't return.

It is important to remember that we are not in control of the events or activities that happen in our life. We are totally in control of our reactions and behaviors. Our reactions to events are based on our maturity levels. Each event in our life has purpose and meaning for us in our own ability to grow and mature. When we come to the realization that we are on a journey, seeking to find ourselves, we can find it through parenting. Parenting is probably the greatest thing that we can do.

Children are the reflection of ourselves, for they were made from us, given to use to nurture. This great challenge can bring a great deal of meaning and purpose into our lives. It can give us that close unconditional love that we all need. It is love that keeps us strong and healthy. Love is our true self.

As you are parenting, become the thinker – not the doer – for the doer just maintains the self. The doer does not think about his actions or consequences. The thinker, however, evaluates, tries to understand his world, tries to find ways to solve problems and ways to serve himself and serve the children in his family.

The reason I have chosen to stay in education all these years is because I believe that schools are an extension of parenting. Not only do we have the responsibility to educate the children, but we also take on the moral responsibility to help children mature. If children are not getting unconditional love from a parent, then they must find a role model within their lives who can give them this relationship. Therefore, it is so important that somewhere in their lives children find the nurturing and loving relationship. This important relationship will help them mature. All relationships are experiences will help each child to reach his own potential. We have a great opportunity in our educational system. We must choose the finest conscious-level people who can provide that relationship that is so necessary. Although that in itself may not be the sole answer, it certainly will be an important part of the child's life. A teacher can help nurture the child toward his own higher level of maturity.

How we discipline our children is an important aspect of what type of relationship we will have with them and how they will respond to the lessons that we are trying to teach. In school and at home, this same concept should hold true. If a child is punished for his behavior, he is more likely to become fearful and self-protecting. The physical punishment brings upon stress and anxiety; it does not bring upon responsibility for change in the behavior. Punishment serves to control the child by fear. The child will then self-protect and become sneaky and deceptive in order to avoid the punishment.

This only makes the child become angry against the person who punishes him. He seeks revenge for the hurt that has been inflicted upon him. He will not see others as loving and nurturing. He will see a person who comes to punish him. When empathy and concern for the child are shown, the child can learn. The child will learn to live with the consequences of his behavior. The child is still loved. He feels important. The child will take responsibility for his behavior because the child wants to learn from the experiences of his life. If we provide consequences for the behavior instead of punishment for the child the child will learn not to do the things that have caused the consequences.

For example, the child on the playground who does not follow the rules gets angry and trips another child. If that child is then brought in and given a spanking, he will not like the principal and the person who told on him, and be angry and revengeful. He will take the punishment. He will be very blaming and seek to avoid another trip to the principal's office for another paddling. However, if the child is spoken to and is removed from the playground for a period of time knowing full well that it was his own actions that caused his removal, he will have time to think about his behavior and contemplate the consequences which he caused. This child will then learn that people care about him, there is structure and there are rules, and there are consequences for breaking the rules. This child will become more and more responsible for his behavior as he is able to handle the consequences. There is no fear that there will be physical punishment.

Although punishment is expedient and demoralizing it does not help the child to mature. There are many good resources on discipline and parenting skills that are available in bookstores.

The second aspect of discipline and control is structure. Structure is very important. A child needs to know the boundaries. He needs to know what is expected of him. Structure and boundaries must be followed consistently. The parent must be able to check systematically on the child even at times hoping to catch the child not conforming to structure. It is early in life that we can teach the lessons needed so that the child will become responsible. The structure must be one that you can live with and to which the child can conform. The rules should be fair and consistent. The child should know exactly where the lines are drawn. If this takes place, the child will then learn to fit into the structure, conform and obey the rules. This will be a safe environment, one that still has freedom of choice for the child, yet boundaries that keep him moving in the direction of learning to be responsible.

Both parents should decide what the boundaries are. They should work towards consistency. Both parents should conform to the structure consistently so the child has consistent enforcement of the rules. There is a tremendous time commitment in parenting. Parents must adjust to the many demands of raising a family. Successful parents take on all the responsibilities of nurturing and raising children to insure they will become mature adults. It takes great love and self-sacrifice.

The conscious person seems to have more energy. He manages his time and meets his own needs. Serving others with his time and energy is his focus. This is not to say that one should give up meeting his own needs. The child learns to meet his needs by seeing that you meet yours. Nurturing parents do not solve all the problems for the child but allow the child to solve his own problems. You are there for consultation and nurturing. You are there because you love the child. The child must feel your unconditional love. It is up to you to provide the environment in which to grow.

The relationship of a child and his parent is a life long relationship. Parenting does not end as our children get older. We should continue working on our relationship with our children throughout our entire life. Any wounds that we have caused need to be healed. Our relationship needs to continue to grow. We must not isolate ourselves from our families.

The stronger the family is the easier life's obstacles are to overcome. It is in the hard times that we reach to the relationships that we have in order to pull us through the situations that sometimes become difficult.

In the upcoming chapter on transition we will discuss the many aspects that could help each adult as well as our children to mature. It is a never-ending process – one that we must work on throughout our entire life. If you are a parent – be proud! Give it your best shot. Put your best effort and energy toward the children that you have brought into this world. To be a parent is the greatest service one can give.

Chapter 2

Transition

I n the chapter on parenting, we discussed the natural growth of the child. We looked at conditions that are necessary for the maturity of that child. When a person becomes an adult and has had trauma throughout their childhood, growth may be very difficult. If unconditional love from both parents has not been there, we hurt. If one or the other parent has subjected the child to neglect, abuse and/or abandonment, the child remains angry. In adulthood, we are faced with a world that is complicated and difficult. We need to have reached a level of maturation that will allow us self-confidence. Then we can be successful.

In this chapter on transition we will explore ways for an adult to achieve maturity. We must grow in our awareness of self. We need to develop the skills that will make a difference in our growth. Maturity is the key to success, well-being and growth.

I have found through the years of counseling and working with adults that the lower maturity stages are very difficult in which to initiate change. If the egotists of our world reach adulthood, they are more often locked away in our institutions, either mental hospitals or prisons. They are taken out of the mainstream of society. Either they have met with tragic deaths, or we have removed them for their behavior. They remain self-confined in a world that is lonely and one that continues to blame an uncaring world.

Many people with social problems such as drug addiction, alcoholism, eating disorders or obesity remain in their maturity between the self-confined and the conventional stage. They are at a transition point in their lives. Yet when they are abusive to themselves by abusing drugs or alcohol, they revert to the lower maturity level of being more and more self-confined.

It is my experience that these people are very difficult to work with yet there are programs that do help them. One of my observations in working with alcoholics is that when they have finally reached rock bottom and are about to lose everything that they have in life – when the thread between life and death is very thin there comes a moment when they realize that the world is bigger than them. They then make that transition to a consciousness. They become aware of other people in their lives. They are ready to move forward in their maturity. This sometimes is a life-long process. These people are sometimes only given one chance for growth.

What works for them is that for the first time they have found meaning and purpose greater than themselves. Through organizations such as Alcoholics Anonymous they are able to find unconditional love from a support group who is ready and able to help them always – 24 hours a day, 7 days a week – during their recovery. These groups are successful because they band together with a meaning and purpose. They have had similar experiences, and know how lonely and difficult a road of growth is. These organizations are successful because they are there for each other and they bond together. This person, for the first time, has other human beings caring for them deeply. They begin to move forward, especially in the cases when the families have been loving all along. The alcoholic for the first time has the love returned as the person becomes aware of his family.

If you are faced with a person who is self-confined in your life and you are seeking to help him, professional help is a route that each of us should seek. It is very difficult for us to help the self-confined adult move forward. They are blaming, self-protective and irresponsible. It is difficult for them to take the necessary steps to self-evaluate. Without self-evaluation, they will not grow.

I do not believe that a self-confined person would take interest in a book such as this, for they believe that they are okay. His world is right within himself. It is other people that are to blame for any problems he encounters.

Transition is easiest for those who have reached the conventional stage of maturity. Although they are still reluctant to take responsibility at times, they at times see a world that is bigger than them. Therefore, the transitional techniques will work best on the individuals who have matured to a conventional stage.

I believe the greatest population is in the conventional stage. The most good can be done for people that are seeking to grown and mature. If you want to find your true self, then you have probably already reached at least the conventional stage. This does not mean that we aren't concerned about the egotist and the self-confined; we should continue all resources available to us to help these people grow. We should analyze our institutions, our prisons and the techniques we use to help these people grow. It is my intent that this book will help the people who are at a conventional level grow and mature. We can change our society, the way we think, where we put our energies so that we can help the greater mankind.

What techniques and ideas can help people grow and mature to find their true self? The conventional person conforms to group norms. If this book becomes something that people are reading and learning from, then this person may be the one to go out and buy to conform to what other people are thinking and doing. It may be the 'popular' book to buy. That need to belong and be accepted is so important to them. Their desire for social acceptability is high – they want to fit it – so they would be open at this time. Hopefully, as they are reading an analyzing their own level of maturity, there is a new awareness - a consciousness of themselves.

Once we have identified where we are functioning, we can replace the lower, immature behavior with mature behavior. That behavior is more helpful and healthier for our own self-concepts.

With information about our maturity, the subjective/objective tug of war can become more objective and we are able to make that first transition of being able to self-evaluate. If we can evaluate our own behavior, analyze it, and find where the behavior comes from, then there are things that we can do to promote growth within ourselves.

There is no way of truly knowing where any of us lie in our maturity. It is only up to us to seek to find within ourselves where we believe we can grow. I have hesitated throughout all this development of this concept to label stages because no one person fits into any one stage totally. We are constantly in transition, constantly growing. We fluctuate in our behavior, for sometimes we act self-confined for a moment and then grow back to a more conventional or conscious level. Yet trying to label these and put them in categories would only serve to help identify where we are functioning. Again, it is a roadmap for us to use to evaluate ourselves – road signs – hints to ourselves – directions to follow so that we may become more mature in our behavior.

When an individual wants to grow, the first technique for transition is to find meaning and purpose in one's life. We must search within ourselves for the purpose for existence. Why is it important for me to be on this earth? A living body, living out a life – what is my purpose? Do I have a mission? How can I be of service? As thoughts come to me, I become aware of what I believe my purpose to be. I must seek out these thoughts and form a statement of purpose within my own mind.

To find meaning is sometimes difficult in a world that demands so much of us. However, meaning can be the energy that drives us toward a greater purpose. Sometimes a sense of meaningless comes over us, and we feel lost. Have we lost sight of any meaning of our life? Search again within yourself to discover and redefine what is meaningful to you. Let your thoughts center on things and events and people who bring meaning to your life.

As you contemplate meaning in your life, give each thought consideration. What is important to me? How does it affect my life? At the end of your exercise, try to find the meaning in your life. Try to bring forth a clear purpose for existence. Identify the people, activities and goals you have that are significant. Give purpose to your life. Purpose in itself will help you move toward a greater awareness of the world in which you live. It will help focus yourself on other people. Events in your life that are important will be helpful to your own growth. Stop concentrating on your daily needs. Too many people are confined to a world of narcissism, of self-confinement, and of egotism. Replace these with purpose and meaning.

Fear is one of the most negative and destructive emotions we have. Yet we live in a world controlled and directed by fear. Fear is an emotion that was never meant to limit us. Fear can be so destructive in our lives. Fear was given to us as a protective defense to keep us safe from physical danger. It is important to replace fear within your own feelings and emotions with what I call the '4 C's' – *Concern, Caution* and *Careful Consideration.*

It is important to be concerned about safely- safety in your home and work place. Have concern for your family and friends' safety, but do not fear that something bad will happen. It is important to use caution in making decisions. Gather all information available to you when making decisions. Do not allow the feeling of fear to control your decisions. When you are making changes in you life, making choices or acting on request, give careful consideration. Never feel pressure that comes from fear. Be confident that you will make good decisions, choices and changes in your life because of the '4 C's'. Do not allow a negative event to be drawn to you out of fear. Feel love and warmth flowing through you with a competence that fear is no longer a part of your life. Use the 4 C's to replace fear. Fear is a negative aspect in our lives. When you have cast out fear, you will no longer be reluctant to try things. You won't be afraid or fretful. This in itself moves us toward a higher level of consciousness.

Transition is attained more quickly by thankfulness. It is important to develop a feeling and attitude of being thankful for your existence. It is an opportunity for spiritual and personal growth. We are a gift from the entire universe: we are love from a loving Father. We need to develop an all-embracing love. I must be thankful for all that I have and all that I am becoming. I am thankful for all the events in my life as they help me grow closer to my Creator.

Concentrate and visualize the people for whom you are thankful for and for whom you show love. See in your mind the people who have done good things for you. Remember people you care about and whom you have given many wonderful experiences. Thankfulness will give you energy. You will become aware of a larger world.

Concentrate on family and friends, a former teacher, neighbor or an acquaintance, fellow workers or school mates. Visualize those that come to your mind and be thankful for them. For it is through thanksgiving that we realize our greater self and our greater purpose.

We are often quick to judge other people, yet we will seldom self-evaluate. A helpful practice for transition is to suspend judgment before participating in an event or an activity, workshop or outing. Think about the attitude of suspending judgment until the entire event is over. Keep an open mind so that you can gain from the experience. Say to yourself, "I will to judge or evaluate the upcoming event until I am completely through the event and have had time to reflect. If I evaluate too soon because I am uncomfortable or unsure of how this could benefit me, it will change the course of the whole experience. If I judge too soon, I may miss out on the benefits that the event has to offer."

All life experiences, with the right attitude, can be positive in terms of personal growth, no matter how painful or unpleasant the experience may be. The first part of the experience may not go well, yet the total experience may be wonderful and helpful if we ride out the tide of events. Suspend judgment, for it may be the key to your own personal growth.

I told my wife of this exercise before she was to go on a 50-mile wilderness hike several years ago. She flew out to Oregon leaving our two boys and me. After she had been there 24 hours, just before the hike was to begin, she was ready to turn around and come back for she was lonely. The experience did not seem very worthwhile at the time, but she remembered my words and persevered and tried to suspend judgment. Upon returning from the five-day women's hike through the Oregon wilderness area, she came back feeling the hike was one of the most important experiences in growth in her entire life. Had she gone with her impulsive feelings and fear and returned home, she would not have experienced the wonderful growth and fellowship that took place.

There are many examples of how people have persevered through experiences and grown a great deal. It is through this technique that we can face events in our life. We can grow from experiencing them if we have the state of mind and the maturity to suspend judgment.

We all have painful experiences from time to time. We all have tasks that we do not want to take on, confrontations with people that we do not want to be involved in, things which we would rather leave left undone and avoid. When you are faced with a painful experience, try not to avoid it – running from it only to meet it again when it has growth. The next time you meet it, it becomes even more ugly with greater energy and more potential for harm. Meet the tough decisions and experiences head-on as soon as you can. Take the attitude that you can face your daily problems and that you can grow from the pain.

After you have been successful in meeting a painful experience head-on, and being successful with it, reward yourself with the energy that comes from victory over difficult situations. Do not be reluctant. Take the energy; do not avoid the pain, for it can be an experience of growth for you.

Remember that strength and courage are attributes of a mature person. We find ourselves fearful and reluctant in painful situations. Draw from that natural inner strength, take courage and be successful and victorious over the painful events in your life.

I see life as a journey, traveling through time, gaining experience from events in our lives. But, I believe that we have control over the events that come in our lives. Visions of life experiences are important. It is important to visualize yourself in experiences that are pleasant and important to you. Visualization and thoughts are creations being sent out that work toward manifesting those very thoughts that we have. If we can see ourselves five, ten or even forth years from now, then we will work toward accomplishing those goals and making those events happen.

I often visualize what I want to be doing and experiencing in the years to come. What people will be sharing my life? Can I see them clearly in my vision? I focus on the events, one by one, seeing them clearly, looking for details, feelings and emotions that I will have during the experiences. This vision should be one that is clear, one that has purpose and meaning for you, one that you truly want to accomplish. Vision will program your mind to work toward those thoughts, for those thoughts are a part of creation. The architect who designs and sees the building that will be built will then later see it become a reality through that visualization – through the creative thought that has been set out on paper for the contractors to build.

I believe success comes from those thoughts and visions that we have. Transition can take place and growth will be experienced when we can visualize the events that we want to have happen in our lives. That is what we will work for, and sooner or later, they will become a reality. Patience and the nurturing of our goals will cause them to come about.

Giving up hope, having doubts, or having fears are the destructors of the vision that we have created. Exercising the removal of fear in our lives will bring about the visions and the realities for which we hope.

I have already discussed being reluctant. Reluctance is a very dangerous behavior to have because it keeps us from our growth. When you feel reluctant to assert yourself, when you are uneasy about phoning someone or talking to someone about a concern, visualize yourself in that situation. Say to yourself, "I am competent and capable, I shall speak clearly and carefully in order to discuss my concern. Both parties will win and gain from the verbal exchange. I feel good that I have solved my problem directly and showed mature behavior. I did not avoid what I thought might be an unpleasant experience. I feel myself growing and becoming more competent. I have set myself apart form the situation in order to converse and understand the other person, solve a problem, or discuss a concern openly and honestly with feelings that both parties can gain from the experience. I feel good about my assertiveness and know that I will not be reluctant in situations to come. I will be capable of handling problems."

This exercise done consistently over a period of time will help make transition possible and aid in your maturity. We discussed somewhat in the visualization that patience is important. You know it takes a few months to grow a squash, it takes 100 years to grow a sturdy oak tree standing tall and majestic. If our visualizations are goals and visions that we have for ourselves are to come about, we must develop the skill of patience. Patience is the key concept for those thoughts to mature and manifest themselves in our world. Patience is the energy that is becoming, without it dreams and goals cannot be realized. You must keep the thought in your mind that you must display patience. Being impatient gains nothing and only patience allows the dream to become a reality.

I am reminded of the gardener who plants the bean in the ground, waters it, the sun pours its energy into the ground and warms it, the sun pours its energy into the ground and warms it, and germination takes place. However, the gardener becomes impatient, it has not grown, and he stops watering. Yet just below the crust of the earth, the seed is ready to burst forth the very next day. But the gardener gives up and walks away, the soil hardens, and the seed dies beneath the soil.

Patience is so important in our lives, for that is what helps us grow. The mature person displays a great deal of patience in his life and therefore his vision and his goals are manifested. The impulsive person does not allow his visions to be manifested, but aimlessly wanders from one thing to another, never allowing any of it to grow or mature.

Objectivity is a sign of maturity. It is not very easy for us, since we are self-centered by our beginnings. Our goal is to mature toward a selflessness. It is important to practice objectivity in situations in our lives. When you are too close or personally involved in the situation and cannot see the whole picture or make a good decision, you have probably become to subjective. It is important to say to yourself, "I must be objective—remove myself from the situation in order to see both sides of the issue and make a fair and reasonable decision about my thoughts and actions."

Ask yourself, "Have I shown empathy and understanding for the other person's feelings in this situation? How are they affected? Can I put myself in their shoes? How would I feel? What could happen that could make the situation a win-win for all involved?"

Contemplate and be objective. Seek a solution that is good for both parties. Seek to help the other person and yourself by bringing a resolution in which both can benefit. Yes, we need to protect ourselves and be concerned about things in our lives, but it is so important to be able to be objective and see the needs of other people. We must seek to serve others. In our service, it will come back to us, and our needs will be met as well. Practicing objectivity will bring about a transition to a more mature person.

One of the strongest emotions that we have in our life is anger. Anger is so destructive to relationships and to the visions and ideas for ourselves. No person ever causes us to become angry. We become angry because of emotions and feelings that are laden in our memories. The only way that I have found to remove them from our subconscious and our memories, is through forgiveness—forgiveness of self and others. Search for forgiveness whenever anger is involved. If a person is finding that he is often angry and is struggling with anger, then it is important for that person to seek professional help. These techniques only work if a person can truly find the source of anger. If not, the person may need help in searching for the cause.

When we become angry, we must remember that it is important to control our emotions. We must take responsibility for our temper and know that the recent event that made us angry did not cause the anger, but only triggered a hurt within ourselves. Searching for the root of the anger is important. If we are to curb the anger, heal it, and have it return no more, we must forgive the original person who caused the hurt. It is important to find forgiveness for yourself or for the person that had any part in the original anger. It should be healed and forgiven. A true emotional healing is needed, not just as intellectual understanding.

Often the hurt is hidden deep in our subconscious and cannot be exposed. If per chance you become aware of a person who has caused you pain, you can meditate on that person. Find within your own heart to embrace the person in meditation. Visualize the person, telling them that you love them, and that you can forgive them.

It is also important to ask the person that you have become angry with to forgive you. In forgiveness there is healing on both parts. Then you are free of the anger and able to move on. Anger will come less often when it is accompanied with forgiveness. Try to always find the source of your anger.

A listing of resources is provided in the appendix of this book for those who wish to seek additional help when it becomes necessary in their lives.

I think we are all aware of a higher source and that, through guidance, we can sometimes make better decisions if we allow our intuition to guide us. After considering all available information on a problem, person, or situation, before making a decision, let your intuition guide you, and guide your final action. Say to yourself, "I am removing myself from the problem, situation, and person. I am clearing my mind of all thoughts about the matter. I am allowing the inner spirit of my being to speak to me and give me guidance. I am confident that I have sought the best solution given all information, in allowing my inner self and my intuition to guide me. The answers may not come to me immediately, but I will be aware of my inner soul. It will speak to me, and I will wait patently until the answer comes, like a light turning on a darkened room."

Intuition can play an important part in our lives. It can help us make decisions that are important and give us guidance. These techniques can be helpful in making the transitions through the stages of maturity. One of the most important elements is the person's willingness and desire to grow. We are comfortable where we are and are reluctant to move forward. But, if we don't move forward, we will never find the many great treasures that are ahead of us. It is through our own perseverance, our own patience, and our willingness to self-evaluate that we can begin to grow and mature.

It is so vitally important that the human race grows, for we are still very primitive in our consciousness and our awareness of our true self. Searching for ourselves is so important. We have not found the true nature of our being on this planet but continue to destroy it daily, we continue to destroy each other daily. There is such a need for a heightened consciousness and awareness of the many problems of the world. I could write a whole book on just the problems of the world, which would solve nothing. If we are able to move ourselves from a conventional, accepting, conforming stage of maturity to the higher levels of consciousness and autonomy, then we can easily and quickly solve the problems of the world. There are so few at a high level of maturity. Truly autonomous and mature people are hard to find. We need leaders and role models who are mature. There are masses that are still confided to a lower level of maturity, yet they cannot do it alone, for each individual's soul has a great deal of energy and power. The lower levels of maturity are working against the forces that are trying to solve and help the people of our world. If we allow the self-confined and the egotists to be the leaders, to control the world in a self-serving way, it will bring all us to our knees. Many environmentalists and humanists believe that there is such a fine thread between existence and non-existence. We have already destroyed many species of animals in our world. The same situation can happen to all species—even if one species is lost.

We are connected by a source of energy that comes from our creator. Whatever religion or philosophy one may have, our existence is real, we are here inhabiting a planet, trying to grow and find ourselves. We must seek to find ourselves quickly, growing and maturing so that we can solve our problems. If we do not mature, then we will be doomed as some of the species on our planet already have been.

The problems that we have are great. The human race can and will mature. We must be patient and persevere, and we must work on our relationships. As I move to the next chapter, I will continue to discuss the importance of relationships and what can be done to help us as a human race.

Chapter 3

Young Love

D uring my ten years as a high school teacher and counselor, I had many opportunities to discuss relationships with young people. Most people reach
the conventional stage by the ages of 16 through 22. During that time, we have
the very strong need to have a positive relationship. Chances are, however, we
often settle for a negative relationship. We are not yet ready in our own maturity
to self-evaluate and evaluate the intentions of others.

There is so much excitement in young love and such a need for that positive
relationship that we often overlook our princesses and knights in shining armor
for the real true selves. The person who is still functioning at the self-confined
level (not revealing his/her true self by deception) can allow us to be fooled into
a relationship that can end in sorrow and frustration. In order for us to discern
the real person, it is helpful to look at the stages of maturity in relationship to
ourselves and to the people to whom we relate.

It is my hope that when you understand the importance of maturity in your
relationships, it will be easier for you to let go of the negative relationships and
have the patience to wait for that true, caring, loving relationship that is just
around the corner.

Use the stages of maturity to guide you. Look for the maturity level in which
you are functioning as well as the level of the person to whom you are relating.
If you discover that she/he is in the lower levels (being deceitful and /or angry at
times) that she/he is overly jealous, superficial in his/her niceness to you, and

only seeking to serve him(her)self, be aware that sooner or later you will discover the true self.

Use the higher levels of behavior for yourself. Give yourself patience and time; be able to evaluate yourself, and be comfortable with yourself. Do not hurry the relationship. Time is an element that helps us discover the strength of our relationship. Relationships should grow strong. If you see fights, disagreements, and/or discord, it is a red flag.

Many young people play a game in a relationship that children play on the playground called "Capture the Flag." As soon as somebody has captured another person's love and acceptance, then it is to be thrown away, and the game goes on. This is a very immature, self-serving type of relationship. The person who is playing this game is extremely self-confined person. In order to have a strong relationship, you must first become comfortable with yourself. Spend time alone. Love yourself. It is only after you have a strong self-concept and high self-esteem that you can love another person. Seek first to understand your own needs and your own strengths before pulling in another relationship that may only confuse the already troubled self.

As you are looking for a possible mate, look for the strong mature relationship in your life. Young love is extremely exciting, full of energy, and full of commitment. Yet, it is a high that comes down quickly when it is built on false impressions. You need to give the relationship time enough to mature, to fully understand the other person in his/her own complexities. A historical tradition of courtship is not so far out of line, even today in our modern society.

Young people still need guidance of more mature adults to help them discern relationships and find the truth in them. In our loving eyes, we often mask our true feelings because of our strong desires to be accepted and to have a positive relationship with another person. I think it is important to keep that tradition of guidance through courtship alive. It may be old-fashioned, yet the maturity levels of our young people would not indicate that they have the tools to discern a relationship in which they are so highly involved. They cannot remain objective in such an emotionally charged relationship. They need the subjectivity of their parents and friends in order to make sure that the decisions they are making will be good, lifetime decisions: ones that they will not regret later in hardship, anger, and failure.

A relationship that fails brings a great deal of pain. This experience can often be extremely violent, angry and painful. The individuals in a lower maturity level will have threats, violence, and anger. We read in the paper each day of the domestic violence and anger that comes from divorce; even violent death can result.

So, if you are a young person involved in a relationship reading this and thinking that you do not need the guidance of your parents or your friends, think again. It is so important for you to make the right decisions in your relationships and to see the true person. Their eyes can be much more open and objective. Listen to their concerns about your relationship. Allow them to understand and know your concerns. Discuss relationships openly and honestly with not only your friends and the person you are involved with, but also with your parents. Having had many relationships over their years, they have a great deal of wisdom. People who love you only want the best for you.

A hurried relationship may result in an untimely end. I have often told my psychology classes that when you see the other person using behaviors such as bribery, jealousy, and/or trying to control/manipulate you, these are signs of immaturity and unwillingness to give unconditionally to you. Don't be afraid to end a relationship out of fear. The conventional person is reluctant to speak his/her mind, to pull out of a relationship, to perhaps hurt another person. Yet, truth is extremely important in a relationship. Each person should honestly and openly share how she/he is feeling about the relationship so that the other person can adjust to the relationship or that both of you will discover that the relationship should end.

As young people move into their adulthood, which in our society is 21, and they are in college, it is acceptable for them to make all of their own choices. Yet, at times, young people put themselves in very serious situations—dating on a regular basis, not knowing the person well, being alone with someone too soon or getting intimately involved too soon. It is appalling in our society to see the numbers of date rapes in college. It is extremely high. People are putting themselves into situations where they cannot control or know the person they are with because of an accepted conformity to an expectation of sexual encounters with very little relationship.

It is extremely prudent to take a great deal of caution when one is in the dating scene. It is important to take time to get to know each other before the relationship speeds up and involves intimate situations. Even at the adult level, it is easy to become involved in an affair that ends in despair and violence. The popular movie "Fatal Attraction" is an example of an extreme case of an egotistic, psychotic attachment to another person. To a much lesser degree, many relationships can evolve in this type of capture and control. Proceed with caution in relationships and use the stages of maturity to judge your own abilities and the strength and maturity of the people with whom you become involved.

As maturity takes a great deal of experience and the growth is often extremely slow, it is important to understand that your love and your perception of the love of the other person will not, in itself, cause the other person to grow rapidly in his/her maturity. You get what you see. If there are many things about the other person that you do not like and you think that you can quickly change them after marriage, closer involvement, or that your love alone will cause rapid growth, think again. This is an idealistic view that many young people have. It's been proven time and time again through the divorce courts that this change did not happen.

One of the most important behaviors that one can use in relationships is intuition. Intuition is a gift. Allow it to guide you. If you feel good about a relationship, continue. If you do not feel good about a relationship, break it off quickly, as more involvement will only cause complications in the relationship. Do not be deceived. The closer you get, the harder it is to get the person out of your life.

Something my father told me about relationships when I was young is to look at the parents of the person you are involved with. If you are a girl involved with a boy, look at the mother relationship. Is there a positive, open, strong relationship with his mother, or is the mother smothering the boy, giving in to every need and expecting no responsibility? If the latter is the case, you will find a person who is typically immature and expecting the same thing out of a wife. But, if you find a positive, loving relationship where the son has taken responsibility for himself and has matured and has a loving caring relationship with his mother, sister, and/or other women in his life, then that is the type of relationship you can expect. That relationship is conditioned, and that maturity has been built over his lifetime. It will not easily be changed with his involvement with you.

The same is true for the boy who is looking for a girl. It is very important that the girl has had other positive relationships in her life, starting with her father. As she was raised, the positive strokes and the impressions she has of the memory of her childhood with her father or brother are very important in how she will relate to you. If she had a loving unconditional love from her father, one that nurtured her along, told her she was pretty when she was young, that she was capable and strong, then you can expect the continued strength in relationships with males will be there when you enter into a long-term relationship.

This is not always the case, because a person can mature through other relationships in his/her life. But it is certainly a scale by which to acquire a general impression of whether or not this person has had a positive relationship with the opposite sex. The long relationships they have had over many years are an accurate way of looking at how they relate to other people.

We know *how* to have good relationships by having *had* good relationships. If we have failed in our relationships and do not understand why, then we will probably continue to fail in relationships. It is important to search for yourself and discover your own insecurities, your own lack of maturity, and the lack of maturity in others. After that, you can expect accurate perceptions and understand the work your relationship will take in order to maintain positive, loving, and caring.

Enjoy all of your relationships when you are young. They are extremely important in your own personal growth and development. Do not be afraid to have many relationships. Friends are the most important relationships we can have. Often the most enduring and intimate relationships have started out from friendships. A friendship allows you the time to know the person well, to become comfortable, and to enjoy the companionship without moving so quickly into the romance and intimacy that many relationships demand.

If you are a parent, encourage your children to have good, close relationships. If you are a young person seeking a relationship, take it slow, be a friend, get to know the person well, and allow the relationship to mature in a slow but positive way. An important exercise that I tell young people when they are searching for a relationship but haven't found one is to visualize your true ideal. Think about the characteristics you want in a person—the likes and dislikes and life goals you might have. Write them down and describe the person in detail.

You will send out psychic seeds to be planted which will also draw the person who seeks the same toward you. I believe you will attract that person to you. It is an important exercise that will allow you to focus on those true behaviors, the true maturity and goals you find important.

There is a movie that I often recommend to young people who have been searching for quite awhile and not yet found their true ideal. It is a movie called "Made in Heaven". It is about a couple that meets in heaven but were born in different parts of the United States. The story tells of them searching for each other. It also gives you an idea of relationships, how they can end, and how eventually one can find that true, loving relationship for which they have been searching.

When looking for a new car most people don't buy the first car they see. They research and find the one that fits their needs and their purposes. The same is true in a mate. Don't buy the first one that comes along because of a high sales pitch. Let's bring back the tradition of courtship, of long engagements, of time to get to know and trust the person in your relationship.

Studying the maturity levels will help you discover your own levels. Knowing where you are will help you in your perceptions of others and your ability to find, maintain, and hold a wonderful loving positive relationship. Enduring intimate, loving relationships is the most important aspect of our lives. We must search within ourselves to know our own strengths and needs in order to be successful in those relationships.

When you are young and impatient, seek to find the patience and insight and use that intuition to guide you to that positive, loving relationship that you deserve.

Chapter 4

Marriage and Divorce

All humans seem to find themselves in one type of relationship or another. There is a natural instinctive drive to mate and come together in an intimate relationship with another human being. We are most familiar in our culture and society to come together in a marriage relationship. Men and woman join in order to serve each other as helpmates.

It is a natural instinctive drive to feel the warmth and love of another person in a relationship. Although there are other relationships that are found in our society and culture today, the one that I will deal with this in this book is marriage. A man and a woman come together to bond themselves as one for the purpose of survival of our race. They come together to help each other throughout their lives.

When a courtship begins and two people find each other, it is often time and circumstances that bring them together. It has often been said what attracts one to another seldom bind them together. Couples must be very careful why they come together in their relationship. When we are young, we have all the desires and needs within us that draw us to another person. Often what we do not have is the maturity or responsibility in the relationship to make it work. This is why we find so many divorces throughout our society.

This chapter will first focus on the marriage relationship and the importance of it, and then what causes a marriage to fail.

Stages of maturity can give us a great deal of insight to our relationships with other people, help us evaluate those relationships, and grow in them. When the wedding bells are ringing loud and clear and we enter a church, synagogue, or courtroom to unite ourselves with another person, we often find ourselves being very idealistic. Many wonderful vows are taken and many scriptures are read. One most often read is Corinthians 13, which is a wonderful chapter that describes the most mature love possible.

The problems begin as we face the realities of day-to-day living. We cannot live up to our own idealistic expectations because our maturity level just isn't there yet. We envision a loving relationship that is kind and forgiving, one that sees the other person first, and one that seeks to serve the other person in everything that they do. Our maturity level limits us in realizing our full potential in a relationship. Marriage is one of the most important relationships we can have. In marriage, we can either find ourselves faced with a person who reflects our fears and anger, or a person who reflects our love and understanding. Both of these occurrences can take place in a relationship. The importance is to identify the differences, find forgiveness, love, and persevere through the relationship, so that true intimacy may be found. If we are successful in our marriage and find the love that we need in a relationship that has meaning and purpose, then we can relate to others as well. It is in marriage that we learn how to be close and intimate with another person. We carry this knowledge over to the relationship with our children and other important people in our lives.

In summary, it is very important to be successful in our marriage because that is the foundation for all other relationships.

A marriage will only work when two people who have joined continue to keep their vows to work at the relationship. It only takes one to decide to go astray. That leaves the other helpless, now knowing how or what to do to keep the relationship alive. The most important element is the commitment that each makes to continue to work through the relationship when the difficult times come. Either you can find strength in each other, or you can find despair and rejection.

Marriage holds many wonderful experiences. It also can be very difficult and challenging. It is up to us in our relationships to help each other. If you are using the stages of maturity and find yourself displaying a lower behavior, you can use whatever resources you need to persevere and grow to become a more loving person in the relationship. If both people are dedicated to this goal, then each day they will grow stronger in their relationship. They will find the energy and love that dwells within each of us to grow through the relationship, making it stronger and more vital.

Our mates can truly be helpful to us. They can serve our basic needs of love, belonging, purpose and meaning. Without our mates, our lives can be empty and self-indulged without the ability to give unconditionally to another person.

In a later chapter, we will discuss unconditional love. This is the most important element in a marriage relationship—giving to your spouse unconditionally, regardless of what they give to you. Unconditional love means that there are no conditions. This is the element that is necessary for a marriage to be successful. We must strive to grow through our maturity and through a relationship that is strong and loving. Marriage offers this challenge to us, for mates can either reflect our own projected hurt and anger, or mates can return the love and understanding. We must follow the words in Corinthians 13 and be kind and patient, seeking to serve the other person rather than our self.

Together, we must seek the root of our hurt and anger. Together, we must find forgiveness for our self and others. We can grow strong in our relationship. If we continue to provide a model for each other and a sounding board that helps us understand ourselves, nurturing can take place. As we are searching for that true self, that natural love, we can find it through the relationship we have with our mates.

As we talked in the chapter on parenting, when children come along in a marriage, they bring much stress and hard work. If the relationship is sound, together the couple can meet the challenge of parenting. Without the strong bond and love, it will break down through the hardships and struggles of raising children. If it is a mature love, a strong one bonding each together, the family as a unit will be strong, will survive the hardships, and will endure through the difficult times.

There are many stories across the nation, and we see it daily in our newspaper, of people who have come together in strong relationships and have miraculously conquered many obstacles. We should take time to reflect on our own lives. It is helpful to see the need for a strong bonding relationship between our mates. Our vows should be renewed daily, weekly, monthly. They are not to be said and forgotten. They are to be lived. We all need someone who can help us grow.

Divorce comes about when people give up. Blaming each other for the failed marriage shows a lack of maturity. Each has not shown enough patience to allow the relationship to mature. When couples are impulsive, fearful, and lash out at each other, the relationship suffers great damage. Each person becomes angry. The memories and wounds from their childhood have not yet been healed. Each person feels that his mate is the cause of the despair. They are so provoked by the other person, that the wounds become deeper. They then manifest the same hurt on to their mates. One or the other become weary and tired, the pressure and stress of a marriage that is not working becomes unbearable, and one or the other leaves, leaving failure and rejection for the other.

Divorce can be one of the most devastating and hurtful events that can take place in one's life. It is truly an overwhelming hurt to find that the love you have been seeking from the other can't be given. The rejection is deep and is difficult to respond to. A marriage that is not working, a marriage that does not hold love and understanding, a marriage that is full of hate and anger, will end.

When one is faced with divorce, it is a time for searching and a time for a great deal of growth. If we evaluate ourselves at our lowest ebb when we feel rejected and lost through divorce, we may find that our own behaviors and maturity level led to our failure. If we grow through this experience and seek to understand our self and our level of functioning - we can grow in our own maturity. If we have found that we have been selfish and uncaring, that we have been angry and that we hurt, we can seek to find the causes of this. We can grow and prepare our self for a better relationship. However, if we do not, we may wander through many relationships, failing at each of them, for we have not learned, nor have we found the reason for our failures in relationships.

When people find themselves in a divorce situation, it is important to seek counseling. With help we can self-analyze and determine what is left in our lives that is important, then work toward new relationships, choosing relationships with care, finding the mature person that fits our level, so that we can work together to grow in harmony rather than in despair.

As we discussed in transition, it is important to work through the painful times of our lives. Although divorce can be the most painful experience one can endure, it can also be the most growing time. If we take the painful experience and do self-analysis using the concept of stages of maturity to find where we are and then attempt to grow using the transitional techniques, we can make a better relationship for our self in the future.

Marriage is something that should never be taken lightly, although it seems that it is entered into with the idea that if it doesn't work, one can always get out of it and find another relationship. In our culture today, we have made divorce an easy and acceptable thing. Marriage should be seen as something that is greater and more important for survival, for if we are not successful in marriage, our chance of being successful in other relationships is doubtful.

It is then also important that couples that want to enter into a marriage should seek counseling and evaluate their relationship and their reasons and purpose for coming together. They should have common goals and purpose and they should have the conviction that they can make the relationship work. Couples must take responsibility, be conscientious, and work with all the vigor that they can afford to make that relationship work. They will find the gifts of a marriage that can be wonderful indeed. Marriage does hold much love and joy and understanding, a great deal of security and meaning for us all. This institution should be one that we hold high, that we nurture and that we support. In a marriage, it is truly a time when each of us can find ourselves.

As we analyze ourselves and grow, our marriages can become stronger. Our families will be stronger and, therefore, the moral values and the belief systems of our country will grow. We will be able to do more for each other and it will be an insight to our own maturity so that we will grow.

Many times couples come together because of physical attraction. Our sexuality is so important in our relationship, yet a marriage does not survive on sex alone. Each partner seeking to love and serve his mate will find a natural harmony in the intimate relationship, bringing forth joy and bliss. If sex is entered into only out of selfishness and self-gratification, it can be a very harmful experience to the relationship. Sex is an expression of love and intimacy, and a balance should be worked out in any relationship. The male and female are so different in their sexual needs and desires by the physical makeup of their bodies. It is important to understand these differences and work toward the successful harmonious intimate relationship that one can find. The male's sexuality tends to be one of evenness, for he does not go through the same cycle that a female does. He must be able to control his desires to match his mate's. As the female goes through ovulation each month, her desires for sexual relationships are much stronger. However, if that is the only time that two engage in intimacy, it can cause the male to be frustrated and the female to be upset that there is a constant nagging and conflict in this delicate balance.

When one seeks to understand each other's needs, feelings, and emotions, and wants to overcome his own natural tendencies, one can find harmony in intimacy. Each partner should be an engineer, engineering ways to meet the other's needs and still taking care of his own. Through this effort, a great joy can be found, for if one sacrifices himself for the other equally, then both will find the joy and love that can be found in a sexual situation. If sex is only for oneself, it will be but for a moment and not enjoyed in its completeness.

Marriage should be open and honest, and sexual desires and needs should be discussed fully and understood by each. If each seeks to serve the other and help with these problems, a balance can be found and each may enjoy the pleasures of each other physically and emotionally. The relationship will become stronger for the work and the understanding each has displayed.

Marriage can be the most rewarding experience of our lives. It can bring the most purpose and meaning to us. But it is up to both partners who have decided to come together to work diligently at the relationship, finding ways to heal wounds, ways to make the relationship better, being patient and kind, and seeking to serve the other. There is a natural harmony of love between us all, and when that is found in a marriage, true bliss can be discovered.

Chapter 5

Employment and Education

T he greatest challenge to our generation and the generation that we are edu-
cating is to come up with a new educational system that will teach students
to think for themselves rather to be robots who do what they are told. In our
past, we met the needs of an industrial nation which was young and required
people to become skilled in a single activity. The educational system has been a
system that allows children merely to learn a set of skills.

Business and industry are already telling us that the students the educational
system is producing are inadequate and ill prepared to meet the rigorous challenges of a high tech information society. Business and industry no longer want
people who conform in a conventional way to existing standards, but rather need
team players that can think for themselves, make decisions, and become their
own creators. No longer can they be the maintainers and the doers; they must
become the thinker.

This can only happen in a society where the role models of teachers are at a
conscious level of maturity so that thinking, understanding, and becoming responsible will be one of the main goals of our educational system. The question is
asked, "What is wrong with our educational system and why can't it rapidly
change to the needs of our counterparts in the work force?" It is a simple answer,
for the autonomous and conscious mature people have already migrated to the
open challenges of business and industry where salaries are unlimited, where potentials are open, and where people can tap their own resources. The responsible,
thinking, creative people who set ideals and work toward success have filtered

into these areas. Now they are clamoring for other people who can meet those same rigorous standards to come along and fit into business and industry. We are already finding great shortages of people who can fulfill these skills. Unfortunately, our educational system is still full of the conventional that are merely teaching what has been taught them - transmitting down through the generations the same ideas and the same conventional expectations allowing the greatest majority of our population to level off and maintain a conventional level of maturity.

What is needed for our educational system to produce thinkers; people who can take responsibility for their own behavior, who are able to self-evaluate their own standards and make changes in their own lives in order to grow and make a difference in their environment. They are able to build rapport with each other, develop teams, and through those teams, solve problems. Business and industry are using this concept. The Japanese have used it for a long time and have brought it to the United States.

Most Americans have been taught to conform and to think in simplistic, conceptual ideas, to be very expedient and lack patience, wanting things to come for them and have things done for them. They are reluctant to try new things. As we know, in the future we will need to be retrained many times. The conventional person is very reluctant to retrain or learn. This comes very hard for them, for their maturity level will not accept the challenges. They are comfortable and want to remain at the level that they have attained.

So now there is a need for a radical change in the educational system to prepare people to be thinkers and to be at that conscious level of maturity. We must be able to meet the challenges that business and industry have designed for us.

We have left the conventional maturity level to the underdeveloped countries. They are now capable of mass-producing materials by working in factories. We are left with the responsibility of the thinker, of the information processor.

How can we change the educational system around to meet this challenge? I can tell you from my own experience of being in education for 31 years that this will be a difficult change - one that will need the support of business and industry, as well as government because the radical changes that need to take place will not come about in an easy manner. Conventional people who are reluctant to make changes control the system. Change will come slowly without the proper regulations.

The self-protective, conventional educator has been successful in securing his world in many states through what we call a tenure law. After a teacher has reached his/her third year and becomes tenured, it is almost impossible to dismiss the incompetent teacher. Because many of the teachers fit a conventional level does not mean that they can help attain the new skills that are needed in our society. Therefore, they are allowed to remain in their positions and have little influence on the maturity and educational growth of students. They are simply transmitting what has been taught them. They are not the thinker. They are not the role models that are needed in education. Administration is filled with the conventional people, not wanting change, resisting it, even if it comes from the teachers. They are the positions of power. So it will be up to Boards of Education and government legislators to remove the burden of tenure that guarantees a contract for teachers and allows movement within education for the bright, conscious level of maturity to be drawn to the educational ranks.

A conscious person does not want to live or work in an educational environment which restricts the use of materials, restricts the resources because of lack of funding and restricts the autonomy that they are seeking. Autonomy is most important to our most mature people. They need to be able to control their world, manage their ideas and put them into place with their students. The immediate rapport that a higher-maturity person gains with students is one of the most important elements of student success in school. We know that relationship is important, yet if we provide less for them, then they can only work and obtain the model that is presented.

There has been a move in education to select the more competent person. There has been a move to do a better job of evaluation. Yet these are superficial changes. Until we have the most mature people in our educational system, we will not turn out more students who have grown beyond the conventional stage of maturity.

Education must demand that we have the finest and the most mature people in this field. The salaries must be commensurate with the energies, skills, and abilities of the type of people that we need to attract. Education salaries remain lower than its professional counterparts. The reason that most mature educators are in education is not for the money. They would be happier and more content if they were given the autonomy and the materials and support needed to be successful in a classroom. We need to work toward this end if we are to meet the challenges and the needs of the thinking, conscious student who will be able to problem-solve and meet the challenges that business and industry are asking of us. If you study the stages of maturity, you will find that it is the person who reaches at least a conscious level that they are pursued for employment. These skills are necessary to be successful in the society and culture that we have developed.

We need our leaders to take hold and understand what needs to take place in education in order to meet these needs. There is not a simple solution, yet it can be done. Universities need to change their concept and become more responsive. The universities are also full of the conventional that ride on their laurels rather than becoming the thinkers and the innovators. Often they pick up the innovations from the educational system below them, making the changes after it is already slowly taking place below. I previously entered a doctoral program and found that it was just as conventional as all the other programs. It could not meet my needs of becoming an individual who was capable of designing his own program for his own needs, but was merely jumping through the hoop that others had prepared. It is a sad commentary on what most of our universities have become.

If we are to make changes in ourselves, then we must make changes in the structure of our educational system. There are many excellent ideas that are surfacing, but they will need the support of the entire community.

The skills needed are no longer simply taught by rote memorization. What we are asking takes development over a lifetime and a student who has reached a level of intelligence can only apply the intelligence in his world through his level of maturity. If one follows these natural stages, designs educational systems, and provides teachers at a level that is commensurate with what is expected, then we truly can make a difference in our educational setting.

There are schools throughout the country that have made changes and who are attaining these results. We need to uses these models and help other educators make changes and understand the need for them.

Employment

What is the employer to do when faced with a need for higher maturity-level people? Although he understands the skills that the candidate must possess, selection is difficult. Some candidates may not have the skills, but have the ability to obtain them quickly.

I have found in working with people that individuals at a conscious level of maturity can change quickly when asked to do so. So if the employer looks for candidates with a higher level of maturity, he would find a person who can think for himself, who can make decisions, who is objective, who will fulfill the needs of the organization, will be retrained quickly, fit in with people, build an instant rapport, and have empathy and concern for his fellow workers. This person will be a team player.

How does one find a limited resource such as a conscious-level maturity person - for they are in the minority? I have used maturity as an indicator for employment over the last 20 years, and during that time, I have been very successful in changing the makeup of my staff by hiring the conscious-level person. When one hires a conscious-level individual, the problems are over, because that person will seek to solve problems in the organization. He will be a team player and make decisions that fit the greater organization. He will not see himself first, but see others and will contribute greatly to the organization. This is what I believe business and industry are asking for.

Understanding the stages of maturity is the first step in the selection process, for if you are able to identify these behaviors in yourself; you will also recognize them in others. Through a lengthy interview process, one can weed out and see through the behaviors of the immature person through his answers to situations that relate to his maturity and investigation into people who have watched him/her perform.

Understanding the concept of Stages of Personal Maturity will greatly enhance your selection process. Although other concerns should be used, such as the skills and education, the background and experience of people, the most important aspect that will bear upon their success in employment is their level of personal maturity. I found this to hold true in the many people who I have selected, evaluated, and worked with. It is the main reason for the development of the stages of personal maturity. It became a necessity to try to understand how I could select the best possible people to be teachers in my building.

Through observation and understanding how difficult and almost impossible it was to move the self-confined or conventional person to improve, to how quickly change could take place with a conscious-level of maturity brought me to the decision to put my energies into selection. I have tried to find the most mature people. This has been the success in my experience in employment, and I am passing it on to you through this chapter hoping that you can understand how easily the stages of maturity can apply to the work force.

I have questions that I have often used in the selection process to help the trained person identify a ballpark figure of where a person may function in his maturity - although there is never any one level or group in which you can place a person. Tendencies can be found which can help show the person's maturity. Again, I caution against judging other people, for this book is sub-titled <u>In Search of Self</u> and not an evaluation of others. Yet it is very important if we are to find the best autonomous people for education that I offer this as a possibility to use in your own selection process. If you are interested a training session in employee selection using the Stages of Personal Maturity process, please contact me at jdreimers@comcast.net.

Train yourself in the understanding of maturity and the importance that it plays upon the success of any organization, and you will find each day that it may ring true to these concepts. In any organization, we can generalize and put people into three categories: the destroyers, the maintainers, and the creators. The egotists and the self-confined are the destroyers, for when you have hired or come in contact with a person at these maturity levels, they will seek to undermine and destroy the organization in which they work. These people usually do not hold onto their jobs very long often before they are dismissed or resign, they have destroyed part of the organization. Certainly, they do not make contributions, but are always asking to have their needs served.

The conventional-level people, who make up most of our population, are the maintainers. They do what they are told and do it cheerfully sometimes. They are, for the most part, easy to get along with yet they simply maintain. The conscious, the autonomous, and the mature levels are creators. They are our thinkers. They are authentic. They manage conflict, they have patience, they self-evaluate, they set long-term goals that they accomplish, they are able to self-evaluate, and they are creative. They are able to have mutual trust and respect among each other. They are empathetic and understanding. They know how to cope with the stresses of our society. They seek to serve other people and have the energy to do so. Their intellectual potentials are beginning to be revealed, as they are thinkers and even knowers at the highest levels. They have discovered something through their own thinking rather than just merely being told. They are able to conceptualize complexly. They can understand a world greater than themselves. This toleration for differences and ambiguity allows them to understand the complex world. Their logic and their common sense applied to their daily lives makes them successful. They are aware of their own intuition and they trust it. They allow the creative thoughts to be formed and become realities. They are disciplined and consistent. They seek self-fulfillment and they enjoy mutual achievements. These are the team players that business and industry want. These are the creators. They have self-respect and dignity. Look for these attributes, and you will have a successful organization.

Sometimes we are fortunate and this mature person comes aboard and makes a great difference. If an organization truly wants to grow, then it must seek to find this level of maturity in order to ensure the success of the organization.

Further training is probably needed to understand the stages of maturity in order to use them in staff selection. It takes an autonomous person with great responsibility that would be careful in his use and understanding of this type of selection process. I maintain the belief that the most powerful selection process is using the Stages of Personal Maturity as an indicator for one's success in the work place.

It has been my experience that this is true, and I believe that others will find so as they begin to understand this concept. , Our earlier discussion has centered on the employer seeking to find the right person. However, if you are an individual who is reading this book for self-improvement, wanting to grow and become more successful, if you want to become the right person, to have those abilities that we have just described, then this is a great opportunity for your own improvement and growth to take place. Now you have a roadmap by which to follow. You can begin to work on your own maturity by using the transitional exercises that are provided at the end of the book in the appendix daily, using the stages of maturity chart as a guide and a map, and practicing those exercises and skills. You will move from the conventional, if that indeed is the level at which you are functioning, toward a more conscious-level and awareness of yourself. Use this guide, for that is what business and industry will be looking for. It is what you are capable of becoming, for it is your natural and instinctive nature to become more conscious and aware. You cannot find that without searching for yourself. Nobody else can tell us where we are or who we are. The conventional methods of handing it down to us through whatever covenant or dogma are not good enough. You must find it yourself—you must find it within yourself, you must turn within, and understand your own behaviors, your own motivations. Visualize your own goals. Be aware of your own personal maturity. I believe we all come from the same creative force of love. We all have the same potential. It is up to us to take control.

We have truly been given the autonomy to make decisions for ourselves, plan improvements, and grow. The concepts of Stages of Personal Maturity were developed for this purpose in mind. It is a roadmap and a guide for us to self-evaluate and make the necessary changes. If we want our children to be successful, we can also follow the levels of personal maturity so that we can become the role models they need. They then can attain a higher level of maturity, but not if we remain at the lower level of maturity ourselves.

If the student is to become greater than the teacher, then the teacher must be able to open the doors for growth to take place. Growth takes place through our relationships. If the son is to become greater than the father, then the father must open the doors and instruct the son so that he may learn from his experiences. We must open the door of opportunity and allow this growth to take place.

Knowing what business and industry are looking for, you must begin now. Knowing the behaviors and the maturity that you must display, move toward a change. Take heart that it is possible, through diligent practice and exercise on a daily basis. I have designed this book with two pullouts. The Stages of Personal Maturity chart can be laid on your desk and viewed on a regular basis. The other is exercise, which can be pulled out and used in your own meditations on a daily basis.

When you meet the challenges that life provides, this can be a guide to help you design your own ways to cope with life's situations. I hope that beyond using this as a guide, you seek the true knowledge within yourself, listening to your own intuitions, listening to that still small voice within you to help guide you. The greatest source of power and energy is already within you. One only needs to go within and allow those forces to work. This concept is not meant to be an end, but a key opening a door to yourself. Continue seeking yourself in a way that will fulfill your greatest vision, for yourself, your family, and your life.

Chapter 6

Death and Dying

Death is a topic that we seldom face or think about until an event in our life forces us to. Either we come face to face with the loss of a loved one who has been close to us, or we find ourselves faced with a disease that may cause our own death.

Facing our mortality is something that is difficult. It is very important to analyze our own thinking and beliefs so we have the maturity to understand the cause and take responsibility for disease and, ultimately, death. We have been told that stress is a killer, that our inability to cope with the conflicts of our daily lives is the true killer. So it would seem that at the higher level of maturity, we would have the abilities to cope and solve problems. This would then enable us to have a longer and healthier life.

My understanding of death came with the loss of my father some ten years ago. He contracted an incurable kidney disease when he was about 66 and died at the age of 70. During those four years was a time of thought and preparation for his passing. My father was the person in my life who gave me unconditional love, who had built that rapport of caring and nurturing with me. Although both of my parents equally shared in my nurturing, my father was the first one for me to lose. Having gained a great deal from that relationship, it was not easy to let go after the death experience. There were many events that followed his death. My feeling of closeness to him never left. This led me to believe that only the physical body had left. His spiritual body continued. There was a oneness between us. Yet that story would take another book to tell, and perhaps someday it can be written.

Before the discussion of death, it is important to bring attention to the growth that takes place through the death experience. Personal growth can take place when we seek to understand our own mortality. Death is but a transition. We can prepare ourselves for death. Earlier in our lives we can prevent an untimely death. Having more time on earth to be in a physical body will give us more time to grow and mature. It is my belief that we are incarnated into a physical being so that we can become more conscious and more mature. It is through the experiences of our life that we can grow.

We must take the attitude that we are responsible for our lives. Events happen through our own actions and thoughts. We can learn to take control and become responsible for our lives. It seems that only people who have reached a conscious level of maturity take that responsibility for their lives. Many people who go to doctors to be healed from diseases do not want to participate in that healing. They only want or expect that they will be healed, healed by the surgery or the drugs that the physician has to offer. Yet the physician played no part in the development of the disease in the individual.

It is my belief that we create our own lives. We reap what we sow. We are responsible for our physical being. The physical being is maintained through our mental and spiritual selves. If we are to maintain a happy, healthy, and fulfilled life, then we must develop to a level of awareness of our own maturity. This maturity allows us to take this responsibility to become conscientious in the care of the physical as well as the spiritual. The two then will be in harmony. The body will be healthy and support our spirit as we are learning and growing in this incarnation in the physical body. We are not our bodies. We are spiritual beings occupying a physical body.

Many people in our society today are suffering from diseases which we have no cure for—cancer, heart disease, and the new virus which is devastating to us—AIDS. Many people are seeking to find a cure. Many turn towards love, trying to take the responsibility for their healing. It is my concern that a disease that has developed in the body over thirty or forty years cannot be changed in a moment. The lack of change and understanding which caused the disease cannot be turned around in the few months and years left in a person's life. He has contracted a disease because of years of neglect.

Disease only dwells in a body that is incapable of fighting it off. The body that is not in harmony that does not have the energy or understanding of the "self" cannot fight it off completely. We have seen miraculous turnabouts when awareness and consciousness have been raised so that the person is beginning to take responsibility. A new awareness comes about them. Many cancers have been reversed and even overcome; yet many haven't. We should take heart in the fact that we area spiritual eternal being continuing to grow and that we should prepare ourselves for the transition. There is life after death. It is a very difficult concept for me to believe that death is final. Energy is eternal, love, which bore us, is eternal and therefore our spirit has a longer journey than just one lifetime.

Although this concept is not greatly accepted, it is illogical for me to believe any other way. It has taken me almost 57 years to make a little growth in my own spiritual and personal maturity. Even by the time that I finish this lifetime, it would be inconceivable for me to believe that I would not still need to work toward my own personal growth in relationship to my own spiritual being.

Stages of maturity for me, is the model that I seek to become. Since my own evaluation of myself, my search, my quest, has found me short of the goal. It is inconceivable for me to believe that I could attain full maturity by only having this life. Whether one believes in reincarnation or not, these same concepts and principles would hold true for either. If we have only one life to live, then it is just as important to continue to grow and mature as far as we possible can, attaining the highest goal that we believe in. However, on the other hand, if we have fallen short and death takes us early, then we can learn from that experience and in turn continue to grow spiritually on our path to understand our self.

To me, In Search of Self is a quest that is eternal. Until we have completed the pattern that has been given to us by many prophets and manifested that ideal into ourselves, then we have fallen short of our true and natural being. With each moment we have on this earth, we must seek to become the mature individual. Our maturity will give us freedom. We will find peacefulness in our own being. Showing strength and courage in the face of adversity will give us control. We see courage in the person who is fighting a disease that has overcome the physi-

71

cal body. The disease, however, cannot overcome the spiritual body. If one demonstrates love and works toward the joyful existence of affirming the self, we can overcome death.

The mature person applies the universal truths in a way that is natural and harmonious. This natural expression of love is what we should seek to become. When we are closest to death, we can also become the closest to life. It is at that moment that we see the two and can feel the necessity for growth within our spiritual self. It is so important to reach the intellectual potential of knowing, knowing our self. We are governed by truth and wisdom through a loving god that has provided the energy that created us. This energy sustains us and gives us the ability and the intellect to perceive our world and make decisions about it. It is our responsibility to control our lives and our destinies. At the point that death takes us, we leave the physical mind behind us, yet the spiritual knowledge within us carries over and our growth continues.

There is a feeling of unity amongst all men, there is that oneness of knowing that we can come together, that we have the same creative love within us and that moment that death takes us, we feel that closeness and that oneness. We should seek to find the oneness with our brothers way before that time. It is in our own evaluation and search for self, when we are young and able to make changes in our maturity, that will allow us to grow stronger. In each life that has been given us, we can continue to grow.

Our prayers and our meditation can guide us, by our thoughtfulness, and by our intellects bearing upon the environment and the world in which we find ourselves. For the truths are easily unlocked if we open ourselves to them.

Organized religion has sought to do this for some time, yet in a way it can trap us at a stage that is very conventional, conforming only to the concepts that have been given to us, stopping our search for our self. Organized religion can give us the structure needed to continue our journey if one realizes the pitfalls of conformity.

If one is truly to become enlightened in this lifetime and reach the stage of maturity, then he must seek the light. He must move away from the dark, self-confined egotist, move toward the light of a conscious and aware person who takes the responsibility to search for himself and find the true nature of his being. Life is a wonderful quest. The quest fills me with energy, as it should each of us as we set about our journey through our lifetime. The tools that we need to be successful are at the higher levels of maturity. We only need to seek them and find them within ourselves, replace the old, selfish, dark ways with new, light, giving ways. This has been taught to us through the philosophers and theologians. It is written in the great books. The content of love and understanding has been given to us in <u>The Bible</u> and it is through those resources that we can continue to search and help us on our quest.

When death takes us, it should be a time for which we are prepared, one that we have anticipated, knowing that we have reached our goals and that we can move forward, letting go of the physical, knowing that we are eternal spirits can allow us the freedom that we need to continue our search.

For me, death could never be final. For the love that I have in my friends and family would bring me to complete despair to believe that it could end and that contact would no longer be gained. If we are to believe that there is truly a oneness amongst all of us, then we can keep that person within our hearts and minds throughout this life. We can continue to grow together in the spirit of love that was given to us from the Creator.

No matter what religion or philosophy we may hold, surely there is knowledge of oneness amongst all men. There is a force greater than us. It is my hope again that the Stages of Personal Maturity can be a guide and assistance in times of struggle and need for us to search for the self. So in the times that we are dying and are hopelessly afraid, that we can find joy and peace in the fact that our spiritual self can transform into a being of love and understanding. If this happens, then death is not a tragedy, yet a stage of transition - of growth that can take place.

Chapter 7

Love

It is my belief that we are created unconditionally out of an orb of love of energy. It has been called "God," "father." Whatever religion or philosophy you may believe, our existence is a reality.

For me, the god and father that I seek has no intention for me other than love. He gives us love unconditionally. This love comes with full energy for creation itself through me in the life that I am living. It is my own responsibility to tap this resource and become aware of my oneness with my father. If God made decisions for each of us, they would not be the ones in which we would suffer and have the toils that are laid upon the world as we see today. There seems to be, at times, more evil and darkness in our world than love and light. The love and light of our own creator is hidden within us, for we have not reached our full potential.

Stages of Personal Maturity is an attempt to help us find that unconditional love. Love is life's purpose. We have an opportunity through a physical being to become aware of a love that bore us.

Throughout philosophy and literature, we see the universal truths coming through, for love has been written about time and time again. So have the forces of darkness. It is the theme that we find in our movies, and in our books, and in our philosophy, and in our religion. Those universal thoughts continue to come through our subconscious, hoping that the seed will manifest itself into a true understanding. God is the natural expression of love. I use the term "love," for it is most universally understood as a power that is unique, a power that all of us seek to understand. We all, at one time or another, can feel love, even if it has been for a brief moment. Many of the toils and tribulations that people feel are because of a lack of love in their life. We discussed in the chapter on parenting the importance of unconditional love. Love is the most important element in the nurturing of a child to adulthood. There are so many incidents in our lives that hate and anger and evil rule over many of our people.

We must find ways to give this unconditional love to ourselves and to the people in our lives and to all mankind throughout our world. Until there is a greater understanding that we are one from the same creator, that love is a universal thought and energy that can manifest itself within each of us, then we will fall short of the goal that is within us. We must continue the search for our own natural self that I believe to be an individualization of love. Love has manifested itself in a physical world, providing the opportunities to perceive and understand, to think, discuss, grow in and learn through the experience that life has to offer us. But we must, again as I have said many times throughout this book, take the responsibility for the search; for the search for "self" is the most important goal that each of us can have. It is truly life's purpose. The love of our father, who shines down on us through the light, can guide us toward that knowledge and understanding that mankind has been seeking.

I can no longer search for love and understanding intellectually. I must go within myself trying to feel the unconditional love for my family, for my two sons and my wife, for my extended family, all of the people that I come in contact with and even greater, all mankind. Each action that I have must be one of love toward others. I must let go of the selfish self that has kept me in the dark for so long; that I must strive toward finding the love that bore me, return to that father, understand the oneness and feel a part of him, allowing that love to manifest it in my life.

When my two sons were born, I felt the power of creation, the birth of an individual who was unique to him, who was on his own path, yet was attached to me for the purpose of love and warmth that we could share. For there is no greater opportunity than to feel the love that I have for my sons and the love that I have for the wife who helped me bring them into this life. If we can nurture them, helping them reach a level of maturity and consciousness, which enables them to become thinkers and knowers, then they too can have an impact on the world. They can find joy, love, and harmony as they do as children playing and enjoying each other. Perhaps they can grow toward their spiritual potential and help others. For the creative life energy that is within them will manifest itself and bring forth great fruits. We know this to be a true concept, for it has proven itself over the ages.

Love endures. Love is the most important thing. St. Paul wrote about it in The Bible in Corinthians. I spoke about that in the relationship to marriage. It is also the most important concept that we should hang on to and seek to find within us. For that power and energy which we call love is so vital to our existence. It is the energy that will solve the world's problems. But in order to love unconditionally is difficult for us, as it goes against the inclinations of serving the "self." It goes against the forces of darkness and evil that seems to perpetuate the egotist and the self-confined beings that are also capable of tremendous energy and destruction. We find it in the many terrorists who play upon the innocent through bombings of airplanes, through bombs in airports, and through the destruction of their fellow man. Only an egotist, one in darkness and despair, could level such wrath on his fellow man. 9/11.

We must be forgiving of those people and help them, through unconditional love, grow towards the light, for we must be models. We cannot succumb to the anger and hatred that they are harboring. We must find within ourselves the love that can forgive and grow within ourselves. We must pray for those who are angry, who are functioning at the lowest level, for in our forgiveness, we can truly grow and be free of the hurt and hatred that they are harboring.

The more I am able to love, the greater harmony I feel amongst my fellow men. The greater opportunities seem to open up, and the energy I have for life seems to renew itself two-fold for each time the feeling is given. Having worked with young children as I did (500 of them) each day, I saw in their faces that unconditional love that they have. Yet, as they grow older, the tough world seems to give them experiences which turn them away from their natural being of love and moves them toward the anger and hurt that they are feeling within their spirit.

We must create an environment within our home and family, within our schools and churches, of love, unconditionally to those around us. When love is given freely and returned freely, there is nothing in this whole universe that can stop it. That is a concept that is in The Bible and in many of the philosophies and teachings, yet rarely do people believe the power that is there for them to tap.

It is my hope that all of us will continue to find a love that is within us. Use your love in the world in which we are living. Then we will become a stronger people. We will be able to solve our many, many problems that plague the earth. Life's greatest purpose is to love. Through love, we will prosper. Peace will become a reality. The model that our creator has given us, Jesus Christ, will become a reality in all of us. Christ's life was to show us the way. He is the light and the way, as it is stated in <u>The Bible</u>, he is the model, the pattern that we can follow. His life was one of unconditional love for everybody around him. His life is the model for us to follow, the pattern we should become. We are capable of becoming that same loving person, for to do less is to fall short of our natural path. Although he was the light and the way and showed us the way, we can do no less than become what he was capable of becoming. We must allow that love to manifest itself in us and become the pattern that is our natural inheritance.

Take the time to affirm the joy and love that bore you. Seek to continue to find the mature, loving person that is within you. Forgive the hurt and anger, replace it with love and joy. Continue to search for the self that is truly one with God. You are capable of being the most loving and caring person. The thoughts of love that you have will become the creation of the future. Life, as we know it, depends on us growing and maturing in ways that fulfill our natural path. Continue to seek and you shall find—find the loving self that is within you.

Love is eternal, and so are we! There is no greater concept than the concept to unconditionally love and feel that energy within us. Use the model and pattern of the mature individual to be our ideal and goal. Then we will have a pattern to shoot for. We will have a goal, an ideal, which we are capable of becoming. The love you have found in others is truly eternal. Seek within your own heart and mind and spirit that oneness and closeness of those who have loved you and you have loved. You will never be absent from that love if you truly open yourself and keep in contact with it. Often we close ourselves out of hurt and out of despair. We must not turn away from the love that we fell within our lives.

Love is the power of creation. It sustains us, and it is that in which we should continue to seek. <u>In Search of Self</u> is a journey towards the oneness of that love that comes from the father who bore us and created us. May you find this love that is within you.

Conclusion

I have attempted to provide a concept in which the individual who is seeking to understand the self can attain personal maturity. Trying to understand ourselves is a great undertaking. <u>In Search of Self</u> has been written in order to provide a sketchy roadmap toward the fulfillment and understanding of what we, as human beings, are truly capable of becoming.

I am sure that there are many inconsistencies in this concept. Attributes of one stage or another could fill over into others. One person may never fit into just one category. We are ever changing. We continue to grow. Sometimes we revert to old behaviors yet try to learn new behaviors. We may function at different levels at different times. It is still my belief that we are focused at one level or another for the most part of our being. Mankind has been given models throughout our existence that would provide a better way of functioning for each of us, a way that gives us the control of our own destinies. We have been given the responsibility for that growth. *Stages of Personal Maturity* allows us to evaluate and analyze the world in which we find ourselves. *Stages of Personal Maturity* can help us understand our existence and give us a concept in which we can explore.

We need a great deal more experiences to truly understand ourselves. There is enough information to suggest that unless we move toward the more mature individual, our planet is in great danger. There is a body of information that shows the overwhelming destruction and the loss that the human race is face with by continuing to destroy the environment. Our physical world gives us the opportunity to grow towards our full potential. We must not destroy this chance.

Slowly destroying the world does show that mankind does have autonomy over the world. If we can destroy the world, we can also maintain it and make it better. Each day, as we analyze and see people functioning in the world, we see both. We see terrorists who are killing and destroying each other, who are destroying not only themselves, but also other innocent people. We see industry and business that are polluting the air, the streams, and the environment in which we live. We see vanishing species of animals. We see our rain forests being destroyed. We see a world that is neglected, which is abused, which is indulged. We see people spending billions of dollars on personal appearance rather than on feeding the hungry.

At times our priorities are so self-serving that it seems mankind is not spiritually growing. Yet, for me, I cannot see total despair. I see our destruction on the television and read about it in the newspapers daily. Within me is knowledge that all of us can truly make a difference. That is why I stay in education. Each child that can be matured to a level of awareness, of consciousness, of autonomy, that one person can make a difference for millions is what I strive for.

Each of those people that we are capable of maturing to a higher level will be the scientists, the doctors, the people who open cures for AIDS, cures for cancer. They will be the environmentalists who will solve the planet's physical problems. They will be the leaders who will find ways of creating peace in the world. These leaders will care more about the love for mankind as a greater whole rather than individual country. People will no longer have prejudice, for as people mature, they will do away with the prejudices, and anger, and hatred for races. They will know that they are all brothers, that there is oneness among all of us. They will feel the love and be more open to it.

So, I cannot be a person who fears the future. I see it as bright. The light of God still shines within each of us. We have the many opportunities within this physical world to grow and mature in spiritual ways.

This book has been written out of my own beliefs and experiences, many of which possibly can be criticized and other examples can be found to the contrary. In Search of Self means just that. You may find differences and other paths than mine. Mine is only to serve for those who need a guide, who want to have the treasure map, a treasure map that is open for your own interpretation and your own design.

It is not meant to be a religion or dogma or an absolute truth. It is only meant to be a guideline, a yardstick by which to measure the self, for it is only within each individual seeking to find himself and take responsibility for his own life that true understanding will come about.

Take time each day to pray and meditate about your life. Be open to the intuition that is within you. Trust it; be aware of it, for it will guide you. Use the techniques and design new ones of your own. Continue to pray unceasingly, for it is through prayer that conditions the mind and helps develop the spirit. Through meditation, you can be open to that intuitive self. Through understanding of others, you can gain empathy that is needed. Forgiveness of self and others is vital in the importance of growth. Get rid of the anger and the heavy-laden memories of your childhood. Negative experiences that we have had cause us to remain in the dark, in the hatreds of the past. Remove them, forgive them, shed them of yourself so that you can grow in the light and love that is there for you to behold.

It is my hope and intent that the design of this book, with the pullout *Stages of Personal Maturity Chart* and the exercises can be used on a daily basis over a lifetime, adding to it your own experiences, your own understanding of self, your own exercise that you need to employ to help your own development. Use your own insight, for it is the best. The only person that I can judge within my life is I. I am in search of myself as you are yours.

Let us take this journey together, allowing the thoughts and understanding that we have to be shared with each other. Let us not reject any ideas but be open to all. Universal truths can come through all of us in many ways and at many different times. Let us walk with each other, hand in hand, through this life. We together can solve the problems and become what we are all capable of becoming—the most mature individuals. When we do, we will see the world transformed into what The Bible has told us, heaven on earth, for that would truly be the goal of all of us—to do away with the dark side and allow the light and loving self to manifest it throughout our world.

There are some bright things to happen in our future and they can come about through our prayer and our unceasing dedication to the love and understanding that we find within ourselves.

Never stop searching because I know you are capable of finding your true self.

Exercise Technique

Find a warm, quiet room. Sit in a chair with your feet flat on the floor, back straight, close eyes, begin with several deep breaths, then begin breathing slowly by counting to four while breathing in through your mouth and counting to three while breathing out through your nose. Say to yourself, "I am calm, relaxed, and at peace with myself and the world." As this calming feeling continues, think of love and light flowing through your entire body. Continue allowing the love and light to flow through your body and feeling at peace. After a few minutes, you can continue in the same manner or begin an exercise.

Exercise Intuition

After considering all the available information on a problem, person, or situation, before making a decision, let your intuition guide your final action. Use the exercise technique to become relaxed and calm. While you're in this state, think to yourself, I am removing myself from the problem, situation, and person. I am clearing my mind of all thoughts concerning the matter. I am allowing the inner spirit of my being to speak to me and give me guidance. I am confident that I have sought the best solution given all information and allowing my inner self and my intuition to guide me. The answer may not come to me immediately, but I will be aware that my inner soul will speak to me, and I will wait patiently until the answer comes like a light turning on in a darkened room.

Exercise Forgiveness

ANGER: I realize I became angry. I want to be in control of my emotions. I am responsible for my temper and know that the recent event did not cause my anger, but only triggered a hurt within myself. I must search for the root of my anger and forgive the original person who caused my hurt. I forgive that person and me for any part. IF an image of the person appears in my meditation, I will embrace the person, tell him that I love him and say to him, "I forgive you." I will also ask the person whom I have become angry with to forgive me. I will continue to follow this exercise in order to control my anger and heal the source of it. I will finish this exercise by allowing light and love to flow throughout my body until I feel peaceful, warm, and calm.

Exercise Objectively, Subjectively

After beginning with the exercise technique, I will say to myself I am aware that I am too closely and personally involved in this situation and cannot see the whole picture or make a good decision. I have become too subjective. I must be objective and remove myself from the situation in order to see both sides of the issue and make a fair and reasonable decision about my thoughts and action. I have shown empathy and understanding for other people's feelings that are part in this situation. How are they affected? Can I put myself in their shoes? How would I feel? What could happen that could make the situation a win-win for all involved? Continue to be objective as you contemplate a solution. Seek to help the other person and yourself by bringing a resolution by which both can be benefited. Continue to pour light and love through your body until you fell at peace and calm.

Exercise Nutrition

KERNAL OF CORN: Look at the kernel of corn. Pick it up, feel how hard it is. Visualize it planted in the ground. It is lifeless, yet great potential lies ahead. It begins to rain, and the kernel absorbs the moisture. Life's energy is released. Watch it; see how it begins to sprout and germinate and send out a root to tap the resources of the earth. The sun begins to shine and warms the soil. Soon a sprout pokes its head out of the ground and begins to grow. The corn stalk grows each day from the moisture and nutrients in the ground and from the warmth of the sun. As it grows taller and taller, watch it move toward the sky. The ears of corn begin to form. There is great nourishment in the kernels of corn and the stalks. Watch them grow taller and taller, six and seven feet. It is time for the corn to be harvested, and it is picked and brought forth. Visualize the corn on the cob being cooked and presented at your table. As you eat the corn, feel the nourishment from the ground and the light and the warmth of the sun that helped it grow. As you digest the corn, think about its nourishment to you and be thankful for the process. End your exercise with allowing the warmth of light and love to flow through you.

Exercise Reluctant

When you feel reluctant to assert yourself, you're uneasy about phoning someone or talking to someone about a concern, visualize yourself in the position where you were reluctant. Say to yourself I am competent and capable. I shall speak clearly and carefully in order to discuss my concern. Both parties will win and gain from the verbal exchange. I feel good that I have solved my problem directly and showed mature behavior. I did not avoid what I thought might be an unpleasant experience. I feel myself growing and becoming more confident. I have set myself apart from the situation in order that I could converse and understand the other person and solve a problem or discuss a concern openly and honestly with feelings that both parties can gain from the experience. I feel good about my assertiveness and know that I will not be reluctant in situations to come, that I will be capable of handling them. Allow love and light to pour through you, and when you are calm, the exercise may end.

Exercise Patience

It takes a few months to grow a squash. Visualize a squash growing in the garden. The squash is growing in a garden next to a tall, sturdy 100-year oak tree standing tall and majestic. An elephant comes along and in a fraction of a second, steps on the squash and smashes it into a pile of worthless mush. The elephant pauses for a moment, and in front of the oak tree, and then walks around the giant tree and makes his way on. What do you want to create, a squash or a sturdy oak tree? I will be patient, for patience is the energy that is becoming. Without it, my dreams and goals cannot be realized. I will calm myself and display great patience. Being impatient gains nothing, and only patience allows the dreams to become a reality. I will contemplate on my inner self-allowing a feeling of calmness and patience to come about me. I will allow light and love to flow through me, and I will feel calm and warm.

Exercise Suspend Judgment

Before participating in an event, activity, workshop, or outing, use this exercise in order to keep an open mind and to gain the most from the experience. After using the exercise technique when I am fully relaxed, I will say to myself, I will not judge or evaluate the upcoming event until I am completely through the event and had time to reflect. If I evaluate too soon because I am uncomfortable or unsure of how this could benefit me, it would change the course of the whole experience and miss the benefits to me. All life experience with the right attitude can be positive in terms of personal growth no matter how painful or unpleasant the experience may be. The first part of the experience may not go well, yet the total experience may be wonderful and helpful if we ride out the type of events. Suspend judgment, for it may be the key to your own personal growth.

Exercise Painful Experience

When I am faced with a painful experience, I will not avoid it. Running from it only to meet it again when it has grown and become even more ugly with greater energy and potential for harm. As I am in my calm, meditated state, I will meet the tough decisions and experiences head on as soon as I can. Visualize a new garden just beginning to grow. The soil is rich, the rain is plentiful, and the sun shines daily. The harvest will be great, but a row of weeds begins to grow alongside the planted crops. Each day you weed the garden and the plants grow larger and larger. When it is time to harvest, the crop is plentiful, and there are no weeds to be found; yet, had you left your garden unattended, allowing the weeds to grow side by side with the crop, they would have choked out the garden, and the yield would have been small in comparison. I will face my daily problems and grow in my pain. Continue to allow the warmth and love to flow through you, remaining calm as you end this exercise.

Exercise Life's Vision

After using the exercise technique when I am warm and calm, feeling great love flowing through me, I will take time to plant the seeds of vision for my experiences that I wish to take place in my life. I will visualize myself in experiences that are pleasant and meaningful to me. I will see myself five, ten, even forty years from now. What do I want to be doing, experiencing? What people will be sharing my life? Can I see them clearly in my vision? Focus on these events one by one, seeing them clearly. Look for details, feelings, and emotions that you'll have during the experiences. As you finish the last vision that you have, clear your mind, relax, and feel calm. Allow the warmth of love and light to flow through you as you end the exercise.

Exercise Fear

Fear is one of the most negative and destructive emotions one can have. Yet we live in a world controlled and directed by fear. Fear is an emotion that was never meant to limit us and be so destructive in our lives. Fear was given to us as a protective defense to keep us safe from physical danger. After I have used the exercise techniques when I am calm and feeling safe and secure, I will say to myself, I will replace fear within my own feelings and emotions with three C's: concern, caution, and careful consideration. I will be concerned about safety in my home and workplace with my family and friends, but I will not fear that something bad will happen. I will use caution in making decisions, gathering all available information to help me in my decision, but I will not allow the feeling of fear to control my decisions. When I'm making changes in my life, making choices, or acting on request, I will give careful consideration. I will, however, never feel pressure, which comes from fear. Cast out all fear. I am confident that

I will make good decisions, choices, and changes in my life because of the three C's. I will now allow negative events to be drawn to me out of fear. I will feel love and warmth flowing through me and the confidence that fear is no longer part of my life. It is not necessary, however, I will be concerned and cautious in my dealings and in my decisions. Finish the exercise by letting the love and warmth continue flowing through you.

Exercise Thankfulness

It is important to me to develop a feeling and attitude of being thankful for my existence. It is an opportunity for spiritual and personal growth. I am a gift from the entire universe; I am love from a loving father. I need to develop an all-embracing love. I must be thankful for all that I have and all that I am becoming. I am thankful for all the events in life as they help me grow closer to my creator. Now, visualizing what I am thankful for, I will show love to the people in my life that I care about and who have given me many wonderful experiences. My family, my friends, a former teacher, a neighbor or acquaintance, fellow workers, school mates. Visualize those that come to your mind and be thankful for them. Allow love and light to pass through their image and feel great thanksgiving for the effect that they have had on your life. Feel the emotions for the part they have played in your life and your own development and give thanks for that loving relationship. Take each individual person one by one as it comes to your mind and pour love and light through him or her. Continue going through the people and giving thanksgiving and rejoicing in the love and joy you feel in the relationships that you have and have had. End your exercise feeling warm and calm, rejoice in your thanksgiving.

Exercise Unconditional Love

Love is the created power in our lives. Love brings forth all life and heals all wounds. I will visualize, one by one, all persons in my life who have given me unconditional love. Think of each person. Feel the love and warmth of their being. Experience the oneness of the love between you. Now move your thoughts and vision to people for whom you feel unconditional love - your children, spouse, other family members, friends. Visualize one by one. See your love like a golden, brilliant light following through them. Think and feel the experience of love without conditions of restraints. Love them for their uniqueness. Continue the flow of love and energy through you until you feel warm, relaxed and at peace. With the knowledge that you are loved greatly and that you can love unconditionally the people in your life.

Exercise Purpose and Meaning

Search within yourself the purpose for which you exist. Why is it important for me to be on this earth? - a living body living out a life. What is my purpose? Do I have a mission? How can I be of service? As thoughts come to me, I become aware of what I believe my purpose to be. Allow these thoughts to form a statement of purpose. My purpose is to:

MEANING: Sometimes a sense of meaningless comes over me, and I have lost sight of meaning in my life. I must search again within myself to discover and redefine what is important to me. Let your thoughts center on things, events, and people who bring meaning to my life. Give each thought consideration. What is meaningful to me? How does it affect my life? At the end of this exercise, list in your mind the things that bring meaning and purpose to your existence. After you have thoroughly discovered meaning and purpose and are clear in your mind and feel warm and comfortable with your thoughts, you may end the exercise.

Exercise Control Over

FEAR – ANXIETY – PANIC ATTACKS: There are events in our lives that can cause great fear. If the fear is left unchecked and goes out of control, it can become generalized. A panic attack comes out of the blue at any moment. It is very debilitating. Here is a plan that can help:

CONTROL OF YOUR BREATHING: First take control of your breathing. Lay on your back with your hand on your diaphragm. Breathe in slowly through your nose as you evenly count to five – filling up your lungs. Slowly let the air out through your mouth while counting to five again. Your body will begin to relax. Continue this exercise for 15-20 minutes and practice this technique as often as possible. You have taken the first step in control by understanding that you can control your breathing. If you can control your breathing, you can control your thinking.

CONTROL OF YOUR THINKING: The next step is to take control of your thinking. Replace the fear and anxiety you are feeling with thoughts of peace, joy and confidence. You have the ability to cast out all fear by thinking positive thoughts. Re-program the automatic response of panic with a response of calm control. THINK POSITIVE THOUGHTS ONLY!

CONTROL OF YOUR LIFE: Don't be reluctant to make changes. Make the changes necessary to take care of yourself physically, mentally and spiritually. You cannot always choose the events in your life; however, you can choose your response to them. Use faith in yourself that the power is already within you to overcome. Do not doubt yourself. Remember: 'perfect love casts out all fear'.
Before, during and after a panic attack, use the deep breathing and positive thinking to control your fear and anxiety. Create a list of positive thoughts that have significant meaning to you that you can carry with you to use as needed.
Prayer is the positive thinking you need to bring forth the power, strength and courage to overcome.
Pray as you deep breathe: "Give me strength, give me courage. Give me peace, give me joy." Say it out loud with every breath and every step you take over and over again. Words are very powerful.

Forgiveness

It is important to forgive any person or persons who are involved in the original event (s) that caused this fear. Visualize the person and the event and say, "I forgive you, I forgive myself, please forgive me." Until forgiveness takes place, you cannot move on. This forgiveness must come from your heart, not just from your mind.

Gratitude

It is very important to be grateful. Show gratitude for the many blessings in your life.

Copy this page and use it as a daily tool:

TAKE CONTROL

OF YOUR BREATHING
OF YOUR THINKING
OF YOUR LIFE
TAKE CONTROL OF YOURSELF

DEEP BREATHING:
ONLY POSITIVE THOUGHTS
I AM LIGHT
I AM LOVE!
I AM OK
I AM _____! (insert your name)

REMEMBER

PERFECT LOVE CASTS OUT ALL FEAR
I AM A CHILD OF GOD!
BE BOLD, BE STRONG, FOR THE LORD THY GOD IS WITH ME.

FORGIVENESS

GRATITUDE- BE THANKFUL
PRAY
ABIDE IN ME, AND I IN THEE LORD
HERE I AM LORD, USE ME

PRAY:
GIVE ME STRENGTH.
GIVE ME COURAGE
SAY WITH EVERY BREATH
AND EVERY STEP
GIVE ME PEACE
GIVE ME JOY
THINK ONLY THE MOST
BEAUTIFUL THINGS POSSIBLE
AND YOU WILL BECOME AS
DIVINELY BEAUTIFUL
AS YOUR THOUGHTS

THE MIND IS THE BUILDER AND
CREATOR. IT IS A PLACE OF ITS
OWN. YOU CAN CREATE HEAVEN
IN HELL, OR HELL IN HEAVEN
GOD HAS GIVEN YOU A GIFT OF
LIGHT THAT IS WITHIN YOU.
SEARCH FOR THIS POWER AND
USE IT TO BUILD YOUR OWN
WONDERFUL LIFE IN CHRIST,
FOR HE IS THE LIGHT

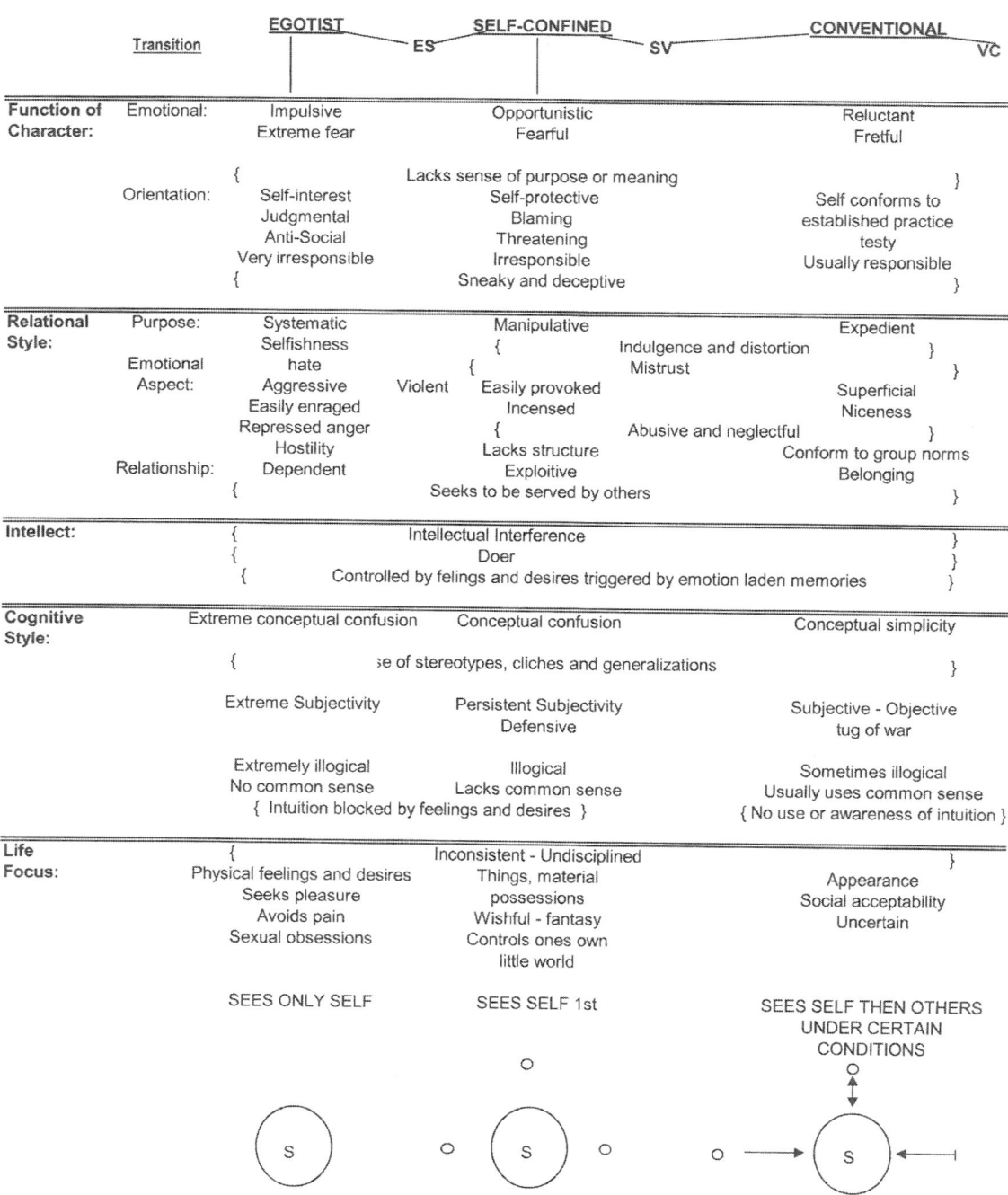

STAGES OF MATURITY (left side of chart)

	Transition	EGOTIST	ES	SELF-CONFINED	SV	CONVENTIONAL	VC
Function of Character:	Emotional:	Impulsive Extreme fear		Opportunistic Fearful		Reluctant Fretful	
	Orientation:	{ Self-interest Judgmental Anti-Social Very irresponsible {		Lacks sense of purpose or meaning Self-protective Blaming Threatening Irresponsible Sneaky and deceptive		Self conforms to established practice testy Usually responsible }	
Relational Style:	Purpose: Emotional Aspect: Relationship:	Systematic Selfishness hate Aggressive Easily enraged Repressed anger Hostility Dependent {	Violent	Manipulative { Indulgence and distortion } { Mistrust } Easily provoked Incensed { Abusive and neglectful } Lacks structure Exploitive Seeks to be served by others		Expedient } Superficial Niceness } Conform to group norms Belonging }	
Intellect:		{ Intellectual Interference } { Doer } { Controlled by felings and desires triggered by emotion laden memories }					
Cognitive Style:		Extreme conceptual confusion { se of stereotypes, cliches and generalizations } Extreme Subjectivity Extremely illogical No common sense { Intuition blocked by feelings and desires }		Conceptual confusion Persistent Subjectivity Defensive Illogical Lacks common sense		Conceptual simplicity Subjective - Objective tug of war Sometimes illogical Usually uses common sense { No use or awareness of intuition }	
Life Focus:		{ Inconsistent - Undisciplined Physical feelings and desires Seeks pleasure Avoids pain Sexual obsessions SEES ONLY SELF		Things, material possessions Wishful - fantasy Controls ones own little world SEES SELF 1st		Appearance Social acceptability Uncertain SEES SELF THEN OTHERS UNDER CERTAIN CONDITIONS	}

John. D. Reimers

92

STAGES OF MATURITY right side of chart

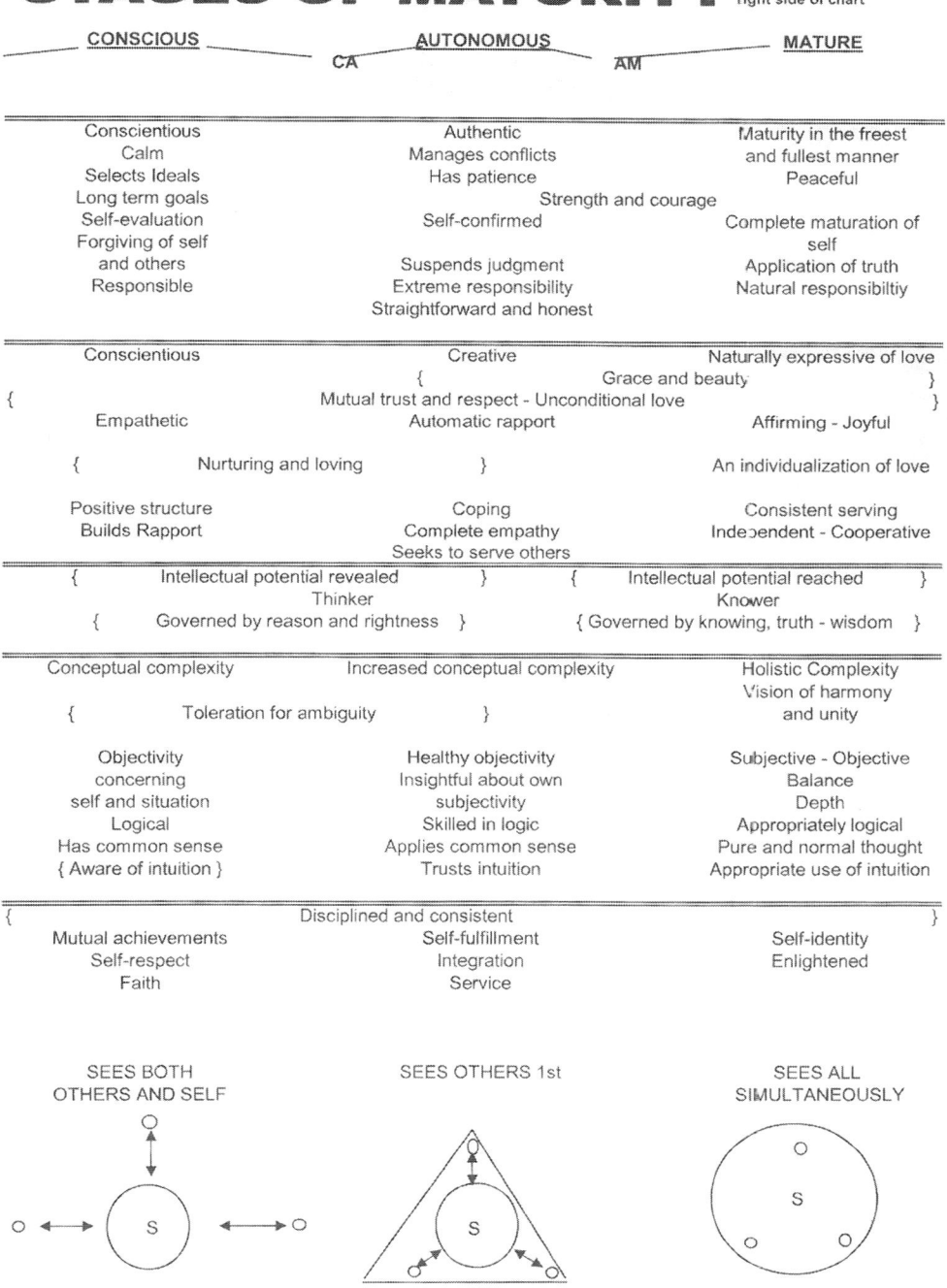

| CONSCIOUS | AUTONOMOUS | MATURE |
CA		AM	
Conscientious	Authentic	Maturity in the freest
Calm	Manages conflicts	and fullest manner
Selects Ideals	Has patience	Peaceful
Long term goals	Strength and courage	
Self-evaluation	Self-confirmed	Complete maturation of
Forgiving of self		self
and others	Suspends judgment	Application of truth
Responsible	Extreme responsibility	Natural responsibiltiy
	Straightforward and honest	
Conscientious	Creative	Naturally expressive of love
	{ Grace and beauty }	}
	Mutual trust and respect - Unconditional love	}
Empathetic	Automatic rapport	Affirming - Joyful
{ Nurturing and loving }		An individualization of love
Positive structure	Coping	Consistent serving
Builds Rapport	Complete empathy	Independent - Cooperative
	Seeks to serve others	
{ Intellectual potential revealed }	{ Intellectual potential reached }
Thinker	Knower
{ Governed by reason and rightness }	{ Governed by knowing, truth - wisdom }
Conceptual complexity	Increased conceptual complexity	Holistic Complexity
		Vision of harmony
{ Toleration for ambiguity }		and unity
Objectivity	Healthy objectivity	Subjective - Objective
concerning	Insightful about own	Balance
self and situation	subjectivity	Depth
Logical	Skilled in logic	Appropriately logical
Has common sense	Applies common sense	Pure and normal thought
{ Aware of intuition }	Trusts intuition	Appropriate use of intuition
{ Disciplined and consistent		}
Mutual achievements	Self-fulfillment	Self-identity
Self-respect	Integration	Enlightened
Faith	Service	

SEES BOTH OTHERS AND SELF	SEES OTHERS 1st	SEES ALL SIMULTANEOUSLY